METAVERSE MASTERY: A COMPREHENSIVE PRACTICAL GUIDE FOR UNDERSTANDING, NAVIGATING AND INVESTING IN THE FUTURE

UNDERSTAND AND PROFIT FROM VIRTUAL WORLDS AND LAND, NFTS, WEB3, BLOCKCHAIN, VR, GAMING, A.I, ART & CRYPTOCURRENCIES

CAMERON BELFORD

SILK PUBLISHING

CONTENTS

INTRODUCTION

You'd be surprised if someone told you that we'd be living entirely in a virtual world in a few years. Almost everything you could do in the real world could be done in the digital world. I'm sure this sounds far-fetched at the moment, but it's going to become a reality in the near future. Buzzwords in the world of technology come and go, but only a select few remain. As technology continues to advance at an ever-increasing rate, so does the list of terms describing it. The "Metaverse," a term coined to describe the virtual realm, is here to stay. You may have heard much about this word in the last few months. The Metaverse is more difficult to explain and comprehend than most technologies because it does not exist in real-time. It's a vision of the internet's future but also a way to keep track of the current state of the internet infrastructure. New businesses and economies have been born due to technological advancements throughout history. With all of its potential, the Metaverse is a game-changer that could fundamentally alter the world.

The AC current, the radio, the cell phone, and the internet all created modern society. While all these technologies were innovative and groundbreaking, no one truly understood them. You can say the same about the Metaverse. The Metaverse is still in its early phases of development, and very few people are aware of what it is. You have a chance to be one of them if you are holding this book; you surely have the desire to know what the future is going to be like. This book can help you grasp what the Metaverse will bring to the world and how everyone will profit from it. The Metaverse will offer a world of possibilities for every individual and business. Knowing about these possibilities might help you keep one step ahead of the competition. If you dismiss it as an internet trend today, you will be left behind when the revolution comes. By the end of this book, you will have a thorough understanding of this futuristic innovation and a variety of methods to invest, earn, and use money in this virtual new world.

I'm an investor myself, and I know how difficult it can be to decide whether you should bet on these new technologies. Crypto, blockchain, NFTs, and Web3 will power the Metaverse. The subject can be complex and confusing. I want to assist you in investing, earning, and using your money wisely. I'm confident the methods, tactics, and concepts provided in this book will help you make better financial decisions and, if used correctly, can help you create a secure financial future. So, what are we waiting for? Let's dive into the Metaverse.

CHAPTER 1
UNDERSTANDING THE METAVERSE

This generation's buzzword may be the Metaverse. It's safe to say that the internet of things will significantly impact our daily lives as we know it. Even though it only became popular on the internet after Facebook changed its name to Meta, experts have been working on it for quite some time. Creating a virtual world may seem new, but it has been around since the early '90s.

WHAT IS A METAVERSE?

To put things into context, what does the term Metaverse mean? Virtual and augmented reality headsets often describe this hypothetical iteration of the internet as one single, universal virtual world. In Time Magazine's definition, the term Metaverse refers to a type of digital community. The current concept of the Metaverse, on the other hand, unifies the digital and physical realms. There are few things that resemble what was imagined in science fiction's early days. This isn't a video game; it's a living, breathing thing. Combinatorial invention: The Metaverse uses a wide range of technologies and trends. We can expect the Internet of Things (IoT), 5G, artificial intelligence (AI), and spatial technologies to all play a significant role in creating this Metaverse through the use of AR, VR, and MR technologies, as well as head-mounted displays (HMDs).

COMPONENTS OF THE METAVERSE

When it comes to creating the Metaverse, multiple technologies will need to work together. All of these technologies must be integrated for the Metaverse to function properly. The following technologies will power the Metaverse:

- Blockchain and Cryptocurrency
- Metaverse Realities
- Artificial Intelligence
- 3D Reconstruction
- Internet of Things (IoT)

Blockchain and Cryptocurrency

Multiple computer network nodes share a decentralized database known as a blockchain. It is possible to think of a blockchain as a digital database because of both store information in a digital format. They offer a more open and decentralized method of proving ownership and transferring value and governance to and from the user community. A cryptocurrency linked to a blockchain, such as Bitcoin, may be familiar to you. The three-dimensional digital realm will be able to transfer value thanks to cryptocurrencies. For example, the in-game cryptocurrency MANA can be used to purchase virtual lands in Decentraland. Using virtual currency, you will be able to purchase land as NFTs. To verify and safeguard the ownership of these NFTs, we will use blockchain technology. The Metaverse, like Decentraland, is expected to run on various cryptocurrencies. These will be used in the Metaverse to buy, sell, and trade digital assets. Both the Metaverse and cryptocurrency are essential components of a decentralized future.

Metaverse Realities

As a virtual world, the Metaverse is expected to be engaging and immersive. It's likely that the technologies that will be the gateways into this virtual world are going to be augmented reality, virtual reality, and mixed reality. Virtual reality and augmented reality allow us to imagine what the Metaverse will look like in the future. A significant portion of the Metaverse's development depends on how these technologies evolve. The Metaverse companies are investing millions of dollars in the development of AR and VR hardware and software because of the enormous potential of both technologies. Later in this book, we will discuss these technologies in greater detail.

Artificial Intelligence

Artificial intelligence (AI) has long been a reality. Among its many applications are business strategy, decision-making complexity, and computing speed. Large amounts of data can be processed in a matter of milliseconds by AI. Artificial intelligence (AI) can be used in the Metaverse as non-player characters (NPCs) (non-player characters). All games have NPCs, which are virtual characters that respond to and interact with the actions of the players. NPCs with artificial intelligence (AI) can also be placed in the 3D digital world to engage in dialogues with users. Similarly, The Metaverse will be a better place as a result of this. This is just one example of how AI can be used in the Metaverse, but it is just one example of how AI can be used in the physical world.

3D Reconstruction

Even though this isn't the first time this has been used, the COVID-19 pandemic pushed it to the forefront of the real estate market, where lockdowns prevented potential buyers from seeing properties in person. Since then, several organizations have emerged to provide virtual tours of real estate using 3D reconstruction technology. It's like the Metaverse in that buyers can look around their new homes from any location and buy them without ever having to set foot inside. One of the Metaverse's primary goals is to create a digital environment that is as close to the real world as possible. However, 3D reconstruction can be used to create scenes that look realistic and natural. With advanced 3D cameras, we can create accurate, photorealistic representations of buildings and other real-world locations. Digital twins, or virtual replicas of real-world objects, are another term for this type of virtual replica.

Internet of Things (IoT)

Connecting the physical world to the Internet via sensors and gadgets is the goal of the Internet of Things (IoT). After connecting to the Internet, these gadgets or devices will have a unique identifier as well as the ability to transfer data. There are now thermostats, medical devices, and voice-activated speakers connected to various data sources via the Internet of Things. An IoT use case in the Metaverse is the collection and distribution of data from the physical world. This would improve the digital representation's accuracy. Certain Metaverse objects' behavior may be affected by IoT data streams, for example, depending on the current weather or other circumstances. Real-world devices can be seamlessly connected to the 3D environment via IoT, the Internet of Things. As a result, it's now possible to run simulations in real-time. The data collected by IoT can be used to improve the Metaverse environment through the application of AI and machine learning.

THE METAVERSE HISTORY

A decentralized new world opens up a slew of new possibilities for individuals, businesses, and the globe as a whole. Although it may seem like a futuristic concept, it has been around for a long time. Snow Crash by Neal Stephenson is where the term Metaverse was first used. When it comes to connecting the physical and digital worlds, this book is your best bet. The novel by Neal Stephenson, published in 1992, is widely regarded as a forerunner in the field.

Electronic goggles and personal terminals similar to today's VR headsets are used to access the virtual world in the novel. Second Life, a virtual online world created by Linden Lab in 2003, made the concept a reality. Although it was inspired by video games like The Sims, this world was nothing like the virtual one. With their daily lives freed, users could escape into elaborate fantasy worlds where they could take on a variety of new identities.

Linden Lab's virtual world attracted 15,000 new members in its first year. As a place to escape reality, the game quickly grew to include in-game currencies, ownership rights, advertisements, and other features. For all their potential, the keyboard and mouse controls were unable to keep up with user demand despite their occasional brilliance. The fact that Second Life was an important first step toward the creation of something like the Metaverse allows us to classify it as such. When Ernest Cline published his dystopian novel Ready Player One in 2009, the world was wracked by social, economic, and climate change issues. The only ideal way to get away from reality is to visit the 'Oasis,' a virtual world. March 29, 2018, marked its release as a film adaptation of this novel, which had previously been published in 2013. This book is being mentioned because of how closely it reflects the current Metaverse vision. With the exception of the book's apocalyptic elements, there are striking similarities between the Metaverse and the Oasis. A taste of what the Metaverse would feel like in its final form was provided. The pioneers of Silicon Valley were inspired by this film/novel. Oculus was purchased by Facebook for $2 billion less than two years after Ready Player One was released on the market.

Oculus was founded by Palmer Luckey, a pioneer in virtual reality. Oculus' acquisition by Facebook (now Meta) was a mystery to everyone. This puzzled me for a couple of reasons. In 2011, virtual reality was not a hot topic, and Facebook was primarily a software company, so it made no sense for them to acquire VR companies. However, no one understood what Zuckerberg's broader vision meant. Zuckerberg appears to have made a significant power move now that it all makes sense, but his critics are worried about how he will interpret the Metaverse. Following this acquisition, businesses became more aware of virtual reality, and things moved faster. Numerous businesses, particularly those in the gaming industry, followed suit and have since introduced new VR and AR experiences into the market. Nintendo, Roblox, and Epic Games are all mentioned. Millions of people wanted to be a part of these AR/VR platforms right away. This showed that consumers have a great deal of interest in the experience of this sort.

However, Microsoft and Meta, two of the most influential tech firms in the world today, provided even more compelling evidence of Metaverse adoption than these video game Metaverses. Known as "Mesh," Microsoft's new mixed reality technology should make working together a lot easier. Similar to the Metaverse, but exclusively for the workplace. HoloLens, a mixed reality headset that will be produced in collaboration with other companies, will be the first to use Mesh. When Meta was renamed from Facebook to Meta, it sparked quite a bit of controversy.

For the Metaverse, a gateway to virtual reality, the company is developing the cheapest and most user-friendly VR headsets. Mark Zuckerberg sees the Metaverse as the Internet's next evolution, and he's willing to invest billions of dollars to make it happen. Over 10,000 people, including some of the best engineers in the world, have already been hired by Meta to work on the Metaverse project.

This is a fascinating concept, but it is still a long way from being realized. However, as with its past, it will be gradually revealed as the most significant invention of the century.

EXAMPLES OF THE METAVERSE

Everyone has heard of the "metaverse," but no one is quite sure what it is. A list of the best platforms or experiences can be difficult to put together because there are so many options. There are some projects that stand out if we define "persistent, connected digital environments that focus on delivering immersive experiences for users" in this context.

Virtual reality, decentralization, and cryptocurrency aren't the only topics covered in this roundup. Even though all of those technologies are likely to find a home in the metaverse, they aren't required in everyone.

As a result, the best examples today tend to focus on those that do one or more of the core elements particularly well rather than those that check all the boxes. This isn't a complete list of all the features that are currently available. All of them, however, give us a glimpse into the digital worlds of the future.

If you've seen the movie or read the book, you'll know that this is a bit of a cheat because it doesn't exist and is entirely fictional. If we're going to be using the metaverse as a way to get away from a bad reality, then this is a great example of what that might look like.

Ready Player One

The movie Ready Player One gives us a glimpse into the near-future world of fully immersive and interactive virtual reality. According to a 2020 Ericsson survey, seven out of ten people believe that by 2030, we will have virtual reality worlds that are indistinguishable from reality. There are many dystopian scenarios in fiction, but this is not one of them, at least in comparison to other fictional digital worlds we could mention.

Second Life

Linden Labs founded Second Life in 2003, long before Facebook (and even before Meta) were even invented. There's some disagreement over whether or not this is truly a metaverse. It's because, as its name implies, it's designed to let users create an alter-ego and live an alternate life online instead of simply bringing their real-world one with them. Alternatively, it could be argued that it was the first widely accepted online metaverse environment. As a useful example of a multi-million user online community with an immersive, hands-on user interface, it may not check all the boxes.

Meta Horizons (Facebook)

A sign of the importance of the metaverse concept to the future of digital communications, socializing, and living, Mark Zuckerberg renamed his company, Meta. Horizon Worlds (a virtual worlds platform), Horizon Venues (an events platform), and Horizon Workrooms (a collaboration platform) have all been developed as a result of this effort (virtual office). When interacting with others on these platforms, avatars that represent users can be used to represent them. As a result of Horizon's existence, we're forced to confront the question of whether we want a metaverse in which ownership and governance are centralized under a corporate owner or distributed and decentralized.

Fortnite

It's no secret that Fortnite is one of the most popular online games ever made, but it's not the only one. But Epic Games quickly realized that once they had brought millions of tech-savvy gamers together on their platform, it could be more game-changing. Live concerts from global superstars like Travis Scott, Ariana Grande, and Billie Eilish are two of the main strands that are being followed in order to transform the world of Fortnite into a proper metaverse. The creative mode has been used by brands such as O2, ITV, and Carrefour to make their first forays into the metaverse.

Decentraland

Decentraland is a web3 platform that straddles the line between a game, a marketing channel, and an experiment in building a digital, decentralized democracy. Decentralized Autonomous Organization (DAO) governs it, and it's home to Morgan Stanley, Coca-Cola, Adidas, Samsung and Snoop Dogg, among other big names. Land there is currently available for purchase for a minimum of $10,000, with the most expensive plots costing well over $1 million in MANA, the region's native cryptocurrency.

Nvidia Omniverse

FOR 3D DESIGNERS, Nvidia's Omniverse is a creative metaverse platform. The Universal Scene Description (USD) language developed by Pixar, a leading animation studio, enables 3D objects and environments to be transferred between different software platforms. Animators, costume designers, and other designers can all work together on a character's face using tools they are already familiar with. As 3D environments become more detailed, immersive, and time-consuming to create, this kind of creative framework will become an essential tool for studios creating metaverse content.

Roblox

More than 50 million people play Roblox every day. In an interconnected metaverse, anyone can create and even monetize their own virtual worlds, complete with avatars and virtual currency. To reach a younger demographic than some of the other platforms mentioned here, brands such as Nike, Forever 21, Gucci, Nascar, Ralph Lauren, and Vans have used the platform to create virtual worlds where users can interact with their brands. However, since anyone can make their own game on the platform, Roblox has made it so that once a user logs in and has a taste for one, they'll be at ease in any of the other games they come across.

The Sandbox

As a mobile game, it was eventually ported to the Ethereum blockchain by the game's developers in 2018, making it one of the first truly decentralized metaverse systems. You can create 3D items, characters, vehicles or anything else you can think of using its own object creation tools that are then minted as NFTs and exported to other Sandbox worlds. The platform's built-in marketplace can also be used to trade and sell these NFTs. SAND is the platform's currency, and like Decentraland, assets and land can be created and traded using NFTs. Companies like HSBC, Warner Music, PwC, and Paris Hilton have all made use of the Sandbox platform to establish a presence in the metaverse.

Otherside

Yuga Labs, the team behind the hugely popular Bored Ape Yacht Club (BAYC) series of NFTs, is working on a metaverse project that has only recently been announced and about which not much is known. The first batch of "deeds" to be sold on the platform raised $285 million in April. The developers of Otherside say, "Players control the world, and their NFTs are playable characters in a metaRPG (role-playing game). Thousands of players can join in real-time."

Pokemon Go

Before the metaverse concept became a hot topic, Pokemon Go was released. There are many reasons why this app is so popular, including the fact that it is a "killer" for augmented reality (AR). One of the best examples of how the metaverse will merge the real and digital worlds is provided by this game. In order to further blur the lines between real-world businesses and the poke-verse, the game's creator Nintendo allowed them to launch advertising and promotion campaigns.

METAVERSE USES

Metaverse technology is already being used by manufacturers to speed up product design, train employees, and improve efficiency. Visitors to the first virtual factory set in a metaverse environment in South Korea can now see plastic screws being manufactured. Visitors to the VR factory can operate virtual machines to make plastic screws in a virtual environment that replicates a real-world factory. It's even possible for them to alter factory settings, such as the production speed.

This type of technology will be extremely beneficial to manufacturing firms in the metaverse future. According to PwC research, the use of VR and AR technology in product and service development alone could lead to an increase in GDP of $360 billion by 2030. Here are some of the ways that manufacturing in the metaverse will be improved by its use.

Product Design Enhancement

The metaverse's virtual world of product design will be enhanced and streamlined by VR and AR. You don't need to conduct costly and time-consuming physical tests to determine whether or not manufacturing certain assets could be made safer or more efficient using digital twin simulations.

A digital twin is a virtual representation of a real-world object. Internet of Things (IoT) sensors collect real-time data from the physical world and send it to computers to recreate as a digital representation in the metaverse to create digital twins. These digital representations can range in size from a single component of a product to a massive warehouse.

Digital twins and metaverse technology can be used by organizations for the following purposes:

- Strategic products can be planned, tested, and built without the worry of costly errors.
- Be on the lookout for potential manufacturing issues before they arise.
- Collaborative workspaces are ideal for creating products.
- Iterate frequently to shorten product lifecycles by incorporating feedback quickly and constantly.

Training Manufacturing Workers Using XR

When it comes to the metaverse, companies plan to use VR and AR technologies to provide immersive training experiences that increase new hire knowledge retention, reduce skill "leakage," and simplify knowledge transfer between teams. Technology conglomerate Honeywell employs immersive virtual reality and augmented reality to enhance training efforts. When employees retire, the company provides them with mixed reality headsets and records exactly what they do at work. The new hires will then be able to see this information overlaid on their own work.

Increasing Productivity and Streamlining Production Methods

Metaverse simulations will allow manufacturers to test thousands of possible factory scenarios and predict the consequences of upscaling or downsizing. Automation and facility optimization can be determined through the use of these simulations by businesses. Technicians are also benefiting from the use of AR technology. In BMW service centers, for example, technicians use AR glasses to complete complex repairs and solve maintenance issues. Video overlays are provided by the glasses, which allow the technician to collaborate with engineers and other experts on the problem.

A virtual factory for electric vehicle drivetrains is also available at BMW, simulating a real-world production line. An entire production line was replicated digitally before building a factory in Bavaria to ensure that all processes were running smoothly.

Improving Quality Control

For quality control and maintenance checks, manufacturers in the metaverse will rely on XR. As a result, they will have lower return rates for defective products and lower maintenance costs because they will be able to identify equipment issues before they become major issues. Airbus, a European aerospace company, is overhauling its military aircraft maintenance inspection process. Drones equipped with high-definition cameras and AR LIDAR sensors conduct fly-around inspections, generating and transmitting data to experts who can detect flaws by examining the data on their tablets and augmented reality spectacles. This new system saves time and minimizes the damage to the aircraft.

Improving Warehouses and Logistics

USING AR, manufacturers in the metaverse will be able to streamline logistics and warehousing processes in the digital world. Among other things, supply chain planning and order picking will become more efficient and accurate in the near future.

As the world's largest logistics service provider, DHL successfully implemented augmented reality (AR) for order picking back in 2015. This new system is now being rolled out across North America by the company. The picking process can be made more efficient and error-free by providing employees with visual cues displayed on glasses as they move through the warehouse.

REMEMBER: This is an exciting time for manufacturing and logistics innovation. By utilizing the metaverse, manufacturers will be able to create products faster, improve product design, increase retention rates through immersive training, and enhance factory and warehouse processes.

THE RELATIONSHIP BETWEEN CRYPTOCURRENCIES, BLOCKCHAIN, AND METAVERSE

Now that you've learned the basics, you're ready to enter the Metaverse on your own computer, tablet, or smartphone. Individuals must also have a virtual wallet with the appropriate cryptocurrency in order to participate in the cryptocurrency market.

However, what is it about it that is so intriguing? The concept and functionality of a virtual wallet are very similar to those of the physical wallets we use to carry cash around with us. The only difference is that "cryptocurrency" is used in the Metaverse, where money is not accurate. You can, however, perform all of the traditional real-world activities with these coins, including selling, buying, storing, and keeping, as well as increasing or decreasing their value.

In other words, the economic transactions we can carry out with euros, dollars, or virtual currencies are identical. The Metaverse has its own currency, called cryptocurrencies, which can be purchased and exchanged there. Real payment instruments that allow for safe, fast, convenient, and anonymous transactions are therefore available. As a result, trades can take place around the world. Because of this, you're able to transcend time and space with ease.

The cryptocurrency system is devoid of the financial intermediaries that inevitably lead to systemic imbalances. The opposite is true in traditional markets, where governments always engage in activities aimed at exerting authority over their citizens. All that's involved are the virtual currency exchange brokers, who deal with the buying and selling for a fee.

This does not mean there is an infinite supply of the coins, nor does it mean that they are constantly being put on sale. To prevent excessive inflation and to ensure that the value of cryptocurrencies does not fall, a maximum quantity has been set in advance for each digital currency (at least for most of them).

This concept can be better understood by drawing a comparison to the real banknotes and coins that we see and handle on a daily basis. Inflation would bring our country to its knees if the Bank of Italy kept printing 5 euro bills indefinitely. Those banknotes would become nothing more than paper with no value. There are a variety of currencies available in the virtual and digital marketplace. You've probably heard of Bitcoin and Ethereum, which are two of the most well-known. There are a lot of cryptocurrencies out there, and new ones are being created all the time. The choice of virtual currency and the method of creating your virtual wallet are two of the most important aspects of living a parallel reality with your alter ego.

This decision must be made carefully and consciously so that you don't end up regretting it in the future. To begin, think about how much money you'll need and where you'll be able to get it. It is important to know the minimum purchase amount, whether the commissions are fixed or variable, how much money you need to invest in the beginning, and which platform to use. Secondly, I recommend that you look into where that currency can be used because you could end up with a cryptocurrency that isn't actually used in your Metaverse.

Cryptocurrencies can be used to conduct economic and commercial transactions in the online world and in the Metaverse. It is referred to as a "block" when one of these transactions is accepted and validated. When a majority of the network's nodes agree that the data is correct, this is referred to as validation. When this occurs, the block is added to the so-called "blockchain," which is a chain made up of all the validated blocks.

In light of this, what exactly is a blockchain? Every successful cryptocurrency exchange transaction is recorded in the blockchain, which functions as a decentralized public ledger. All "miners," or people who work in the virtual market, can access this registry and use it for their own purposes (and, in our specific case, within the Metaverse).

Transactions, on the other hand, are non-reversible. As a result, once an action in your parallel world has been validated, you will be unable to reverse your course. It's possible that all of this will appear overly complicated to you. Even after the initial impact of this system, everything is instantaneous and quick.

As long as all parties involved have access to the data, the blockchain is unquestionably a useful tool for ensuring the integrity of economic transactions. One of the most significant innovations that have been introduced in the modern era is this one, which eliminates the need for an external third party to monitor and control it.

The Metaverse and its cryptocurrencies have been explained, and you may be wondering if it is appropriate and safe to begin trading in this world. There is no doubt in the minds of leading economists and academics that the answer is a resounding yes, for a slew of compelling reasons.

To begin, this new virtual world is a place where you can work, play, and engage in any activity you like. Everyone is also convinced that the Metaverse and economic transactions based on cryptocurrency will be the next frontier for making a lot of money quickly. The data suggests that profits could be very high in the coming months, so they advise investors to start investing and using these cryptocurrencies right away. Even so, some people remain skeptical because, according to some, these cryptocurrencies are only valuable and usable to those who spend their days playing in the Metaverse or on social media.

A virtual wallet with a minimum amount of cryptocurrencies is required to operate in the Metaverse; otherwise, you will not be able to do anything with your avatar in the virtual parallel world. According to a recent study in the United States, the responses of people between the ages of 18 and 55 were predictable. In the first place, younger people are more likely to be interested in operating in the parallel universe and using digital currencies. As a second point, those who are most skeptical of these new horizons believe that these scenarios pose a danger and harm to real life and relationships. Essentially, they believe that people who live in a virtual world are unable to form meaningful relationships with others in the real world.

In addition, Metaverse participants defined it as a possible reality for playing and having fun, but not a world in which to work. Large corporations, such as Amazon, Microsoft, and Apple, have also been a major source of skepticism. Concerns about the impact on the economy and the market have been raised by many. They may be able to take advantage of the Metaverse's evolution to become even richer off the backs of ordinary citizens.

The Metaverse, on the other hand, is a must-have for Generation Z, the next generation, who, when asked, say it is the real evolution of the immediate future. To what extent the parallel world will spread, what it will mean, and how it will influence our traditional economy are all questions that will have to be answered in the future. In other words, is the Metaverse a passing fad or the foundation for the future of commerce and social interaction?

WHY THE METAVERSE WILL BECOME MORE POPULAR NOW

Several of the world's largest technology firms are launching all-out attacks on the metaverse. Microsoft wants to create an enterprise metaverse, while Mark Zuckerberg is all in. Fortnite, Minecraft, and Roblox have already made social gaming a mainstream phenomenon and created platforms that can be used to develop the metaverse. The boxy game beloved by 7 to 12-year-olds, Roblox, may be the most powerful metaverse platform of the future, according to some game developers. The Hadean cloud software powers Minecraft, allowing it to scale to thousands of users per world.

Only recently has the computing power emerged to allow virtual reality to be scaled to a massive scale. Companies like Hadean and Improbable, which specialize in large-scale distributed computing, can get 10,000 players on the same server simultaneously. For a few years now, the idea of holding 50,000-person concerts and sporting events at the same time in the metaverse was unthinkable.

With the advent of cryptocurrencies and non-fungible tokens, the metaverse is now more accessible to businesses looking to expand their operations. As well as allowing you to move your virtual identity and goods between metaverse worlds, these interchangeable tokens will also allow you to use your Roblox pixelated sword as an effective weapon in the Fortnite battle royale.

In Snow Crash and Ready Player One, the metaverse becomes truly "meta," and you are able to hop between platforms in a seamless manner. A similar phenomenon occurred in the 1990s when mobile phones began allowing people to text each other across different networks, and mobile messaging exploded beyond anyone's expectations.

METAVERSE IS MORE THAN JUST A PLACE TO PLAY GAMES

Yes. Playing games in the Metaverse isn't the only way to spend your time there. The obvious place to start is with games, but the metaverse encompasses so much more when viewed from a Web3.0 perspective. Ariana Grande and Travis Scott have performed at Fortnite, while Lil Nas X's Roblox show last year drew 33 million views.

That's why companies like Stage11, based in Paris, are so intriguing. An Otium Capital-funded startup called Stage 11 is developing immersive virtual reality music experiences for the metaverse and has partnered with artists like David Guetta, Snoop Dogg, Ne-Yo and Akon.

Artists of all kinds will create companies that cater to the metaverse, including musicians, fashion designers, and other types of service providers. Gravity Sketch, a company based in London, recently introduced a virtual collaboration room where designers can work remotely on the same 3D design task.

On the more business-oriented side, meetings, education, and healthcare are all possibilities. For example, Warping, a Swedish startup, creates VR training videos for businesses and has worked on a pilot project with digital doctor service Kry to help patients with social anxiety overcome their fears through the use of immersive virtual social scenarios.

A digital twin of a BMW factory created by Nvidia's Omniverse is part of a metaverse. It may be a dull metaverse, but technicians will be able to work together in it, so it's still important.

All companies will have some sort of presence in the metaverse at some point in time, according to Talewind Studios CEO and cofounder Mike Allender. "Right now, every business has a 2D website. There will be a three-dimensional representation of that in the metaverse."

Hundreds of businesses, ranging from early-stage startups to global technology conglomerates, have already established themselves within the metaverse ecosystem.

CHAPTER 2
RISKS AND CHALLENGES OF THE METAVERSE

With VR (Virtual Reality), AR, and MR devices in use, the Metaverse relies heavily on these technologies and devices. The Metaverse, like any new technology, has its share of hurdles to overcome. It is imperative to improve user experience, reduce hardware costs, and enhance software and data processing capabilities in order to meet today's challenges.

As a result, securing the Metaverse will be more difficult than securing current digital platforms, say cyber-security experts and researchers. Similar to the Internet's security, privacy, and safety concerns, the Metaverse will exacerbate these issues even further. In the future, virtual worlds and augmented reality platforms will introduce entirely new security risks and pitfalls for users and businesses alike. There will always be threats to the Metaverse's security, so it's imperative that virtual worlds be built with security in mind from the outset.

Microsoft's corporate vice president of security, compliance, and identity, Vasu Jakkal, says that monitoring and detecting attacks on these new platforms will be "more difficult" than on existing media. As more and more human activity takes place in virtual spaces, the importance of security will only increase. In today's digital world, maintaining security would be a nightmare. A growing number of experts believe that previously unimagined security flaws will become common occurrences and that this will exacerbate the vulnerability of already-vulnerable groups in our digital world already.

In a world where virtual and real worlds continue to blur, many are concerned about the potential dangers that may arise. Rather than removing today's online problems from the news, the Metaverse makes them worse. In light of the revolutionary nature of the Metaverse, a number of legal and regulatory issues are expected.

As a result, it is difficult to determine which jurisdiction and set of laws will apply to the Metaverse. Anticipating and addressing legal and regulatory challenges will be critical if this new parallel world combines technology, content, and human experience as expected. In order to keep consumers safe and ensure fair competition and effective enforcement, its widespread use will expose the public to well-known regulatory loopholes that require immediate attention.

Privacy and age-specific experiences must be addressed immediately by developers. As a result of the lack of precedents and standards, many new legal implications are certain to arise. Unless and until new rules are immediately established.

Unfortunately, consumers in the Metaverse face both traditional marketplace risks (fraud, manipulation, lack of transparency, etc.) and new regulatory gaps in data protection, competition rules, and enforcement/reference jurisprudence opportunities. There are new challenges and adjustments to be made in the regulation and implementation of data protection in the Metaverse.

The scope of rights granted under a license versus those not granted under a license is also an important consideration. Numerous previous controversies have resulted from changes in content use over the last few decades (e.g., CDs, DVDs, digital copies, streaming). They will undoubtedly play an important role in this new virtual environment and may raise additional questions and unique legal issues because of the Metaverse's unique structure. It's been difficult in the past to track down and enforce intellectual property rights in the virtual world, and more of the same is likely.

Virtual and augmented reality, cryptocurrencies, and other elements of the Metaverse have the potential to cause enormous harm, which is why it is so important to create materials and guidelines to help educate the public and families about the dangers of current and future technologies.

According to Stephanie Benoit-Kurtz, a University of Phoenix faculty member and a principal lecturer in the College of Information Systems and Technology, the Metaverse would become more vulnerable to hacking if more hardware was added to support virtual and augmented reality platforms.

THE CONS OF THE METAVERSE

In addition to the positive aspects, there is a dark side to the metaverse. We'll take a closer look at seven potential drawbacks to the metaverse in this post. To create a more immersive digital world for its users, numerous companies are developing apps, products, and services to aid in the development of the metaverse and to serve its users. Metaverse drawbacks must be considered in order to fully comprehend its capabilities. I've compiled a list of the top seven issues facing the metaverse today.

1. Privacy Issues

Metaverse technology allows us to fully immerse ourselves in the digital world, which is the next evolution of the internet. Privacy is becoming a more important concern in the age of digitization. When we go online, we already have privacy concerns in mind. In the metaverse, we can expect the same kinds of tracking technologies that are already in use to monitor our online habits.

Marketers and advertisers, for example, will be able to see from our headset data where and how long we look in our immersive experience if VR headsets include eye-tracking technology. While this is great news for marketers, it's also a major concern for anyone who cares about their personal information.

Wearable and haptic devices that measure our emotions and physical reactions will allow companies to monitor our physical reactions as well. Large amounts of data can be used for marketing or other purposes by companies.

2. Protecting Our Kids

The metaverse will make it even more difficult for parents to keep track of what their children are doing online. Because we can't see what our children are seeing in their VR headsets or monitor their screens on tablets or phones, it will be even more difficult to figure out what they're up to in the metaverse.

3. Health Concerns

VR "hangovers" and "post-VR sadness" are both well-documented phenomena. Returning to reality after being immersed in an amazing virtual world can leave us feeling down and out, and this is only going to become more common as virtual worlds become increasingly realistic. A growing number of children and adults are developing Internet or gaming addictions, and this could become even more of a problem if we become addicted to the metaverse.

4. Access Inequality

A high-tech headset is required for augmented reality experiences, as well as a high-speed internet connection for virtual reality (VR). How can we ensure that the metaverse is accessible to everyone, not just those with the most money and those in the most developed nations? As the importance of these immersive experiences grows, we'll need strategies for expanding people's access to the metaverse.

5. Metaverse Laws

Is it possible to commit a crime in a virtual world? New gray areas in many laws will be introduced as a result of the metaverse. In other words, how is it any different from a real-world assault if someone touches you in virtual reality while you're wearing a haptic suit? As technology advances and complex legal issues arise, we will be forced to deal with these regulatory challenges.

6. Desensitization

Many people will be playing violent games in virtual reality, where you can actually feel and see what you're doing at the same time. People may become less aware of their own actions as a result of these lifelike simulations, which may make them more likely to repeat them. Due to virtual reality desensitization, I believe there is a real risk that people will become more likely to engage in violent or threatening behavior in the real world.

7. Identity Hacking

People will be able to hack our avatars and steal our online identities in the virtual world, where avatars will be used. For example, the hacker could pose as you and cause havoc in both your virtual and real worlds if this were to occur. To reduce virtual reality-related cybercrime, we must find ways to verify identities and avoid deepfakes in the metaverse.

8. Misinformation

The fact that companies like Facebook are pouring money into the development of new metaverse technology is ironic because these same companies are the source of tens of thousands of cases of misinformation or fake news. In the run-up to the 2020 U.S. presidential election, Facebook, in particular, has struggled with fake news. When creating a metaverse, it's important to think about how misinformation might spread in a virtual world.

9. Lack of Regulation

A FUTURE METAVERSE would have a similar lack of regulations as the internet does today, making it easy to imagine. Legal disputes over intellectual property ownership or privacy can both be exacerbated by the lack of regulations. Profit regulations and taxation can also pose a threat. It is imperative that regulations are put in place to deal with cryptocurrency and the revenue streams that it generates for current metaverse companies like online games. To deal with a future metaverse, many governments around the world have not yet modernized their legal infrastructure.

10. Mind games

The bleakest aspect of the metaverse is that it could have a negative effect on its users' mental well-being. Harassment is an issue that virtual environment creators will have to deal with right away. Current methods of physical exploitation in virtual reality are sexual harassment and abuse, which are often aided by weak or absent safety settings. In virtual environments, this has been a longstanding problem, and there are many ways to address it. Immersion in virtual worlds for an extended period of time may also lead to other kinds of mental health problems.

During her time at VR platform Sansar, former Linden Lab security chief Pearlman experienced what she called "phantom timeline syndrome," in which the boundaries between the virtual and real worlds blurred.

"You can't tell the difference between reality and virtual reality," Pearlman said. "When you exit VR, you still feel like you're in a virtual world." She warned that this would be especially harmful to children who are adapting to the metaverse as they grow older. Children are spending a lot of time on virtual and augmented reality platforms, and Pearlman fears that attackers could use misinformation to influence them.

There is also the risk of identity theft and unauthorized access to private information. Children's privacy would be jeopardized if metaverse platforms were able to collect images and other personal information about their users.

Children's privacy becomes even more of a concern when discussing this topic in a public forum. It is inevitable that children will be in this space, and the current Children's Online Privacy Protection Act (COPPA) does not have adequate safeguards in place to deal with the exponential personal information that these environments will collect.

11. Things could get physical

There are bound to be new issues as technology advances and develops. As an example, cyberattacks could move from the digital to the physical realm. Research by Pearlman and his colleagues at XRSI shows how a hacker could manipulate a virtual reality platform to reset the physical boundaries of hardware. Pushing a user into the path of furniture or up a flight of stairs is one example.

It's possible that augmented reality could make this even more dangerous, as users could be misdirected into a dangerous physical situation, such as being kidnapped or robbed. Even worse, the victims of a fictitious attack may feel sick to their stomachs as a result.

"We know that motion sickness can occur in virtual reality," Pearlman said. There is the possibility that a creator could intentionally embed something that causes motion sickness when clicked.

Even more dangerous attacks may be on the horizon, according to Malwarebytes senior threat researcher Christopher Boyd. "As recently as a few years ago, paid advertising was a primary method of monetization in virtual spaces. It's reasonable to expect compromises and rogue ads if regular ad networks with dynamic ad spaces are inserted into games. "SearchSecurity spoke with Boyd, who confirmed the news. As with previous attacks on epilepsy foundations on social media and forums generally, malicious individuals could have substituted regular advertisements with strobing images designed to trigger epileptic seizures."

12. Risks of financial fraud

The first few years of use of the metaverse will see a lot of money moving around. As a result, bank account information, credit card information, and cryptocurrency wallets must all be managed.

13. Behavioral and self-esteem risks

When used as an "escape from reality" for people who want to forget about their problems in the real world, the metaverse can be an illusory way out.

14. Time and Space

Time can be perceived differently in a virtual environment than it is in the real world because users are less aware of their bodies in VR. Users may unintentionally spend more time in the Metaverse as a result of the full immersion. In order to avoid a skewed perception of time, mechanisms must be put in place to keep users in touch with the real world. The concept of space is the second concept that should be examined in the Metaverse. Initially, users may find it difficult to comprehend how much and how much variety there is in the Metaverse because it assumes an infinite space. It will be necessary for Metaverse users to receive guidance on time and space perception in the early stages of immersion in order to ensure they are both aware and comfortable.

15. Community and network

Metaverse is certain to unite a wide range of people from around the world in a single virtual world. Being able to stay in touch has become increasingly important in recent years, and this could lead to the formation of a strong Metaverse network for both professional and personal purposes. Metaverse has the potential to become a place where people can connect and build meaningful relationships. Online communication is already commonplace, but haptic and motion capture technology will need to advance significantly if the Metaverse is to become a place where people can feel both emotionally and physically present. A high level of visual fidelity, combined with the ability to feel and interact with one's environment, allows one to have a full understanding of one's immediate surroundings.

16. Ownership and Property

When we talk about a unified virtual world where you can interact with the world and other people, we can imagine that there will be an opportunity to buy and hold on to various items and assets. In 2021, the popularity of NFTs (Non-Fungible Tokens) was expected to soar, bringing new investors and users to digital assets and tokens. NFTs currently represent real-world objects, granting and proving the ownership rights for art, music, videos and much more. The challenge will be to create a unified system to verify the owners of virtual assets in the Metaverse.

17. Currency and payments systems

Bitcoin is one of the most well-known forms of digital currency that has been around for several decades. Marketplaces like Amazon and eBay, which bring together tens of millions of customers from every continent, are no different. To facilitate quick and hassle-free exchange, Metaverse will undoubtedly have its own version of a virtual marketplace. No matter what currency or marketplace format is used, a brand new transaction verification system will be absolutely critical. The challenge will be convincing Metaverse users that they can rely on and, most importantly, feel safe while engaging in any trade within the virtual world.

18. Reputation and identity

When it comes to the real world, the issue of one's own personal identification and representation is a no-brainer. The Metaverse, on the other hand, raises the question of what constitutes a person's identity in the virtual world. And, perhaps most importantly, how to show that you exist and not some other person or even a bot. Credibility and trustworthiness can both be demonstrated through one's interactions with a reputable organization, and this is where reputation comes into play. Facial features, video, and voice can all be forged, so new methods of verification will inevitably be developed in the near future.

It's clear that the metaverse has a lot of potential issues that need to be addressed (and possibly regulated) as this technology continues to evolve. While we are still at the beginning of our journey into the virtual world, the Metaverse presents both challenges and opportunities. It is absolutely essential to ensure that the Metaverse serves as a complement to the real world rather than a replacement for it. It is important to remain aware, safe, and secure in this new vast universe, even if one is eagerly anticipating the virtual realm.

CHAPTER 3

METAVERSE AND NFTS

In the last few years, you've probably heard about Metaverse and NFT. However, there is still a lot of misinformation out there, so it's important to get educated. Despite what many people believe, there are many uses for blockchain technology that aren't limited to the cryptocurrency sector.

An NFT, in essence, can be squandered in a variety of different ways. In this regard, think of the art world and the sale of all those unique works of art that cannot be owned but are sold at high prices at auctions. In fact, collectors and those with purely speculative interests are becoming increasingly interested in these products.

Metaverses and NFT are already making a significant economic and social impact. Even if NFT isn't real, it's still an attractive asset. You should know that the NFT abbreviation stands for "Non-fungible token," which is used in a variety of contexts. An NFT is basically any item that can be transferred to a new user. The certificate of ownership, on the other hand, does not grant complete freedom to the person who obtains it. NFT owners will be required to adhere to a set of strict rules, including a prohibition on making and selling copies of the object. As a matter of fact, copyright will always be strictly protected.

It's also important to keep in mind that NFT is a synthetic substance, not a natural one. Consequently, any work can be digitized and transformed into something authentic, non-reproducible, and authenticated. In any case, a blockchain-based process will be required to bring the NFT to life. It all comes down to the fees that Ethereum charges, which is widely considered to be the "mother" cryptocurrency along with Bitcoin.

At this point in time, NFTs are in high demand, and not just among collectors and art lovers. In order to understand the consequences of commercialization, you'll need to examine all the features of these certificates of ownership that come with digital works, which are becoming more and more popular.

In fact, if you look closely at NFTs, you'll see that there are other factors to consider besides blockchain technology, such as the trust relationship formed between the buyer and seller. The parties, in fact, believe that the work is unique and will never be sold. To put it simply, the Non-fungible token, which literally translates as "non-copyable token," is something unique; it can never be replaced by another good. To illustrate this point, think about digital currencies that can be traded for each other. Operations that you can't do with a piece of art, a song, or a video game instead.

It's important to remember that when you buy an NFT, you're not actually purchasing a product but rather the copyright and the ability to show it to others. A smart contract will be used to formalize everything. You won't have to worry about the seller and buyer making arbitrary changes. Starting with a photograph or a video, the digital format of the work is created and saved in a special location. When it comes down to computer language, both versions are nothing more than a string of zeros and ones. A hash is a smaller version of the original sequence after it has been appropriately compressed. Despite the fact that the hash can always be calculated, the digital document cannot be reconstructed using the same hash, which is why it's important to mention this now. The time stamp is essential for the next step, which is storing the hash on the blockchain.

After reading this, it is common to wonder how NFT ties into the Metaverse virtual reality. non-fungible tokens allow you to transact in the fascinating Metaverse because they share the same underlying technological foundation.

A more automated market is becoming a reality thanks to the widespread use of these tokens. Cryptocurrencies such as ETH can be used to buy and sell hashes created by the hashing algorithm's creator. A work's creator can be traced within the NFT, and legitimate ownership can be demonstrated accordingly by keeping track of ownership transitions.

The entire mechanism provides proof of the digital work's authenticity and ownership at once. As soon as you own the hash, you have the freedom to demonstrate your rights without relying on third parties or adhering to time constraints. What really matters is whether or not the token's underlying blockchain remains operational.

In order to acquire an NFT, you'll need to use the Ethereum blockchain, which, in most cases, is what you'll find. However, it is important to remember that in the last few months, blockchain (the one that has been used to buy the best NBA plays) and its competitors Binance Smart Chain, EOS, and TRON have also been spreading.

What if you don't know what a blockchain is or how it works? In that case, you'll have to think of it as an enormous database that can't be altered in any way because no one has the right to make changes to the data that is kept inside. Even the state cannot control a blockchain since it is comprised of multiple computers that operate independently of one another. The blockchain will continue to function as long as each computer on the network contributes its efforts.

Once a time stamp has been stored in the blockchain, you can claim ownership of any digitized work, such as a movie or photo. Even if the information is changed or falsified by someone else, no one else will be able to claim the same right. Because the blockchain is both immutable and decentralized, its first use of it was for the benefit of the Bitcoin network. Virtual currency eliminates the possibility of "double spending," i.e., falsification, by enabling safe transactions.

The blockchain has undergone many changes over the years. It has evolved to encompass a wider range of financial transactions, not just currency exchanges. Smart contracts, which are nothing more than decentralized computer products that are extremely reliable because they are based precisely on the blockchain, have been developed specifically for Ethereum since 2015.

This means that smart contracts can only be implemented in accordance with the code that has been made available to the public. No changes or substitutions can be made by a single node in the blockchain network that is not connected. Using NTF smart contracts, it is possible to keep track of the people who create, sell, and purchase smart contracts. Calculating the artwork's hash or numerical sequence is used to do this. When it comes to Ethereum, "ERC-721" or "ERC-1155" is the most widely used and recognized NFT.

As long as the certificate remains unique, it will never change. To host an NFT, Ethereum ensures that the certificate can be modified. However, it will be able to document changes in ownership at the same time.

Now that you know more about NFTs, you only need to look at one to see how sparse and sparsely packed its data is. In order to save energy and maximize storage space, the answer can be found.

If large wires were inserted into the blockchain, they would end up weighing down the entire system, making it extremely difficult to do so. So, now you know why we have to have it hashed.

Are you interested in bidding on an NFT? Your only ownership of the asset is a certificate on the blockchain, where the smart contract identifier is also housed, so you won't actually have any physical access to it once you've been awarded it. Because the certificate does not have a direct connection to the blockchain, the database of certificates simply contains the picture that links to the artwork. The contract terms of the transaction are sometimes referred to in NFTs as well. Alternatively, you can always access the intermediary site to find this vital information.

As you might expect, the system as a whole appears to be quite dependable. Still, there are a few flaws in the system. There are a number of scenarios that could occur if the entire Ethereum blockchain's current community decided to abandon the project. But don't stop there; as time goes on, even hash information will become obsolete. There's a chance that external links to the smart contract's hashes will stop working.

These issues are already being addressed. For those looking to commercialize NFT and conduct business in the Metaverse, a number of technological solutions have been developed to ensure the highest level of security. Some NTFS, for example, use IPFS type addresses to avoid external links that may one day disappear. If the owner of the site stops paying for hosting, or if they need to make room for new content, a URL may be removed. You can always find your content because IPFS addresses are unique to each node on the IPFS network. To ensure that the stored files are accessible and, therefore, long-lasting, a network of hosts has been set up.

Other than Ethereum, the future of individual blockchains is uncertain, but progress is expected because those interested in buying and selling NFTs want more assurances. Pay attention to the blockchain where the smart contracts are hosted when purchasing an NTF. Buying an NTF linked to a blockchain that isn't pre-tested puts you at serious risk of getting a piece of junk with no guarantees. Aim for well-decentralized blockchains that will not be abandoned in the near future.

NFT and the cryptographic Metaverse, a virtual world in which people can interact, have a strong connection because of the blockchain's existence. The Metaverse isn't a standalone system but rather a symbiotic one that connects various digital building blocks. A subcategory is known as PFP, which stands for "Pictures-for-Proof," is a subcategory of NFTs that includes entire collections of images that are exchanged for fun or recreational purposes. All of these unique NFTs are signed by well-known artists from around the world, making them particularly appealing to art collectors.

To put it another way, in the Metaverse, NFTs are a form of ownership documentation.

Since they're so important, many businesses are spending a lot of money on developing encrypted content. Virtual art galleries, open to all players, have already been created in the video game industry to mimic the physical headquarters of manufacturing firms. Attend concerts, participate in various events, and touring rooms are all possibilities for participants.

Coins like Bitcoin and Ethereum can be used to purchase digital works in the Metaverse. In this manner, the seller's ownership of the object will be immediately transferred to the buyer via an NFT. If you'd rather get your hands on the Metaverse, you'll be able to transfer ownership of it this time around as well.

This system's advantages and potential economic impact are self-evident. Because the blockchain in a cryptographic Metaverse is decentralized as opposed to other virtual realities governed by states or other bodies, those who operate within it gain an advantage. If a game hosted in the Metaverse were to be abandoned by the community, it would continue to be visible because of the blockchain's support of the game.

This is an important point to keep in mind: the Metaverse utilizes the same infrastructure as cryptocurrencies and NFTs. When you join the Metaverse, you will become a participant in the crypto-economic network, which is what these terms mean.

As a result, a new economy is emerging, even if some aspects and boundaries have yet to be established. As of right now, the Metaverse presents an exciting opportunity for online promotional activities, particularly in the area of bringing new and alternative ticket sales channels for participation in musical or sporting events to life. Combined with current advertising investments, all of this will undoubtedly lead to increased economic distribution.

The Metaverse's commercial real estate market has seen an increase in recent months in both the buying and selling of these properties. Additionally, a number of high-end fashion brands have made their way into this ever-changing landscape. While this is going on, major technology companies around the world are making significant investments and releasing new flagship products that are specifically targeted at the rapidly expanding digital industry.

Because the global market for NFTs has not yet been fully regulated and many loopholes have yet to be resolved, copyright poses a significant challenge. The parties involved in multi-million dollar transactions are expected to be concerned about possible copyright infringement. The legal protection that is recognized around the world appears to be difficult to obtain at the moment. Ad hoc regulations are required because there are a number of inconsistencies in the laws of the various countries.

There must be a precise definition in order to ensure the long-term viability of both the NFT and the Metaverse by defining what the commercialized work is and, above all, what the external link that refers to the hash is reporting. The link between NFT and the Metaverse is critical to businesses around the world, particularly the big fashion and tech companies. The inability to trade NFTs without first leveraging the blockchain ensures maximum transparency, especially for artists who create captivating and completely novel works.

In any case, it's critical to familiarize yourself with the dynamics of NFTs and the Metaverse before diving in. Do your research and stay up-to-date on the latest developments. Virtual world enthusiasts must be prepared to deal with unpleasant surprises and make purchases without proper consideration. As long as the blockchain is feeding Metaverse finance, cryptocurrency will always be the currency. You can trade digital representations of real-world objects, such as music, art, houses, and entire collections, once you enter the virtual world.

CHAPTER 4

VIRTUAL REALITY

A person can interact with a three-dimensional (3D) visual or sensory artificial environment using computer modeling and simulation in virtual reality (VR). As a result, a virtual world with full 360-degree exploration is created using computer technology. To describe a 3D computer environment that can be explored and interacted with by multiple users, we use the term "virtual reality." This means that virtual reality involves creating a computer-created virtual world that we can interact with in some way. When we talk about "virtual reality," we're referring to a system that uses high-performance computers and special sensory devices like headsets and gloves to simulate parts of our world (or an imagined world).

VR systems currently use electronic helmets to create realistic images, sounds and other sensations that mimic the user's actual physical presence. Users are transported into a 3D environment where they can freely move and interact to complete predefined tasks and achieve goals such as education by designers who create virtual environments such as virtual museums. Virtual reality (VR) creates a computer simulation of an environment in which you are not just a passive participant but also an accomplice using cutting-edge graphics, cutting-edge hardware, and an artistically rendered experience.

With the aid of some sort of input tracking and an eye-tracking monitor, you can immerse yourself in an unreal three-dimensional world created by your computer. Two small, high-resolution OLED or LCD displays, one for each eye, stereoscopic graphics, a binaural sound system, and real-time head position tracking and rotation are all common features of VR helmets. There are many ways to create a virtual world, including interactive games and computer simulations. If we're traveling the world and hoping to see famous landmarks like the Pyramids or intriguing new cities, we're more likely to opt for an augmented reality experience that allows us to see what we see in real-time.

Because we are visual beings, the display technology used in virtual reality differs significantly from that used in traditional user interfaces. An augmented reality app captures digital images rather than taking you into a virtual world. Using a clear viewer or a smartphone, you can see them overlaid on top of the real world. With Mixed Reality (MR), physical and digital objects coexist and interact in real-time in new environments and visualizations that were never possible before.

After that, AR (Augmented Reality) technology overlays the system-generated images with the users' perceptions of the real world on your phone's monitor, making 3D graphics visible directly from the camera's point of view therein.

In this way, a person enters the third dimension and has access to a wide range of capabilities, such as the ability to manipulate objects. Virtual reality could be created by providing one's senses with computer-generated or simulated information, which would alter one's perception of reality.

HISTORY OF VIRTUAL REALITY

The first stereoscope, which used two mirrors to project an image, was developed in 1838. As a result, the first stereoscopes were created. Using two images, these gadgets created a three-dimensional image that appeared to have depth. A 120-degree viewing angle was achieved by using two 2.7-inch diagonal displays. When the US Air Force's first flight simulator was developed in 1966, it sparked the US military's interest in developing virtual simulation systems, which ultimately led to the development of modern virtual reality headsets. There were millions of people around the world who got their first taste of virtual reality gaming thanks to the innovative but far from realistic graphics.

Students of Ivan Sutherland and Ivan Sutherland created the first head-mounted VR/AR display (Sword of Damocles), which was connected to a computer rather than a camera in 1968. When Ivan Sutherland and Bob Sproull presented their prototype of a 3D head-mounted display for virtual and augmented reality in the paper "3D head-mounted display," it was the first head-mounted display for these technologies. In 1955, Morton Heilig proposed a device that could stimulate multiple senses. Morton Heilig, a filmmaker, refined this idea into a patent for the world's first stereoscopic head-mounted display in 1960. Visuals in three dimensions, a wide viewing angle, and true stereo sound are all included.

It was in the '90s that the first mainstream arcade games and virtual reality entertainment systems with multiplayer functionality and a high level of immersion became available, thanks to Virtuality technology. During the early 1990s, the Virtuality Company began mass-producing virtual reality systems and opening virtual reality gaming arcades. Virtual reality gaming, on the other hand, had its defining moment in 1990 with the introduction of high-end arcade machines equipped with HMDs (head-mounted displays).

REAL-WORLD USES OF VIRTUAL REALITY

More uses for virtual reality exist than you might think, from academic research to engineering, design and business. Virtual reality is increasingly being used in the medical industry to train new doctors and experienced surgeons. Virtual reality is being used by medical institutions and universities to teach life-saving procedures to students.

Virtual reality (VR) can help medical students perform real-life operations without risking patients' lives because delicate surgical procedures are time-consuming and dangerous. For mental health issues such as post-traumatic stress disorder and anxiety, virtual reality exposure therapy has been found to be particularly effective.

As a result, trainees can practice more in a safe, virtual environment without putting real patients at risk. A variety of sports can benefit from the use of virtual reality training, which allows coaches and players to watch and experience specific scenarios repeatedly to improve their performance.

With the help of 360-degree frames or real-time 3D rendering environments, virtual reality technology can reproduce authentic restorative experiences (such as Unreal Engine or the Unity real-time rendering engine). Virtual worlds can be created using this technology that mimics real-life situations or creates a virtual world with unrealistic elements, such as in games where players can participate in various situations without risk.

As a result, all possible applications can reduce costs for a variety of purposes, such as employee training or product monitoring as well as item review or project testing. Real estate, for example, makes extensive use of virtual reality (VR). COVID-19 and social isolation sparked a surge in virtual reality use by real estate professionals. Virtual social worlds, accessible via virtual reality, have attracted large numbers of online residents.

There are many well-known examples of virtual social worlds without VR support, including VRChat, Rec Room, AltspaceVR, and Roblox. Many people believe that virtual reality (VR) is only used for gaming or watching movies. Even so, virtual reality (VR) is being used by a slew of businesses, academics, and startups to enhance the lives of millions of people, enhance their products, and conduct ground-breaking research.

Twibi, a digital marketing agency, says that while VR is traditionally associated with the gaming industry, it is unexpectedly being used to control physical environments in various fields. Through the use of virtual reality, users can immerse themselves more deeply in real-world settings. Virtual reality experiences can be created with pre-configured assets and customized to be more interactive using the XR Interaction Toolkit. In the workplace, virtual reality (VR) can be used to give potential employees a taste of what it's like to work in a real-world setting and prepare them to deal with any issues that may arise. When it comes to recruiting and training new employees, some companies are turning to virtual reality.

Toyota even uses Oculus headsets as part of its TeenDrive365 campaign to educate teens and parents to focus their attention away from driving. The automotive industry uses virtual reality for more than just engineering purposes. Virtual reality is seen by automakers as a new means of luring potential customers into dealerships, if only virtually. Virtual reality

For future space missions, astronauts will be trained in robotics using training simulations. To better prepare astronauts for maintenance on board the International Space Station, the agency is utilizing virtual reality helmets. Virtual reality is also used by NASA for astronaut training. There are many companies in the oil, gas and chemical industries that use virtual reality safety training to ensure the safety of their employees before putting them in dangerous situations.

PROS AND CONS OF VIRTUAL REALITY

Virtual reality has the potential to revolutionize our daily routines and improve our quality of life if it is properly implemented. Finally, it can be said that virtual reality is a valuable tool for learning new things, as well as a way to alleviate stress by experiencing positive emotions during visits to virtual worlds designed as works of art. For example, it is already used by many companies to provide a more personalized and intuitive experience to customers and connect people worldwide.

Virtual reality's full potential is being used in a variety of fields, including corporate training, business, combat training, healthcare, education, and the aforementioned gaming technology, among others. The ability to train and practice simulating potentially dangerous real-world operations like surgery, combat, flying, and so on is simply the best practical benefit of VR technology, among the countless other incredible benefits.

Virtual reality technology allows users to feel like they are in real places, hear real sounds, and see real objects. The user can immerse themselves in the game's world through the use of cutting-edge visual effects, audio, and other technologies.

Although touch, smell, and taste are not currently part of the digital experience, they will be in the future. As a result, the full experience of life is diminished. Using virtual reality to communicate should not be used as a replacement for face-to-face interaction. People's vulnerability to deception will be amplified beyond what they currently experience in their interpersonal interactions due to the lack of body language and other means of communication.

Virtual environments and dangers can be explored in a safe environment for students to practice their skills. Students will be better prepared for the real world if they use the software to point out their own mistakes and receive immediate feedback on how to fix them. Students can physically move around and interact with virtual objects in their virtual environment by using handheld VR controllers to lift, push, and pull them. Virtual reality is taking education to new heights.

All of your senses are engrossed in the virtual world of entertainment that the head-up display creates for you. It's possible to design, edit, transform, and test your model in a virtual environment that is full of intricate details and various features. Your workers can experience thousands of situations they wouldn't otherwise be exposed to, such as using expensive equipment for the first time or being put in dangerous situations where their lives are at risk, thanks to virtual reality.

Virtual reality has both advantages and disadvantages:

- Creates a safe learning environment.
- Physical side effects.
- Entertainment.
- Lack of flexibility.
- Helps develop skills.
- High cost.
- Data collection and privacy are at risk.
- Loss of human contact.
- Eliminates language barriers.
- Users become addicted to the virtual world.

It is one of the main drawbacks of gaming that not everyone has access to advanced virtual reality technologies. As the cost of virtual reality devices continues to fall, there is something to be said for this trend. This otherworldly phenomenon will soon be accessible to a broader audience as more and more people have access to virtual reality technology.

KEY ELEMENTS OF VIRTUAL REALITY EXPERIENCE

Virtual worlds, immersion, sensory feedback, and interactivity are all essential components of virtual reality — or any reality, for that matter.

1. Virtual World

For example, a virtual world can only exist in a specific medium. For example, it may exist solely within one person's mind, or it may be broadcast in a way that allows others to access it as well. Similar to how play or film scripts exist outside of the context of the performance of their respective works, a virtual world can exist without being displayed in a VR system (i.e., an integrated collection of hardware, software, and content assembled for producing VR experiences). Virtual worlds are depicted in these scripts. Take this analogy a step further. We can think of a play's script as merely its description. Virtual worlds are created when a play's story is brought to life by actors, sets, and music. Computer-based virtual worlds are similar in that they describe the objects that appear in a simulation. Virtual reality is a term used to describe the experience of seeing that world through a system that brings those objects and interactions to us in a physically immersive, interactive presentation.

2. Immersion

VIRTUAL REALITY CAN BE DEFINED as an immersion into an alternate reality or point of view, given that the user must be completely immersed in the virtual world. However, what does this imply?? What is the best place to immerse yourself in a different reality or perspective? Alternate realities or points of view: what exactly are these things?

A medium meets our definition if its participants are able to perceive something other than what they would normally see or hear without the aid of the medium. These two ways of looking at things are acknowledged by this definition, which acknowledges the possibility of perceiving something other than the reality in which you currently exist.

Alternate worlds can either be a representation of an actual location, or they can be purely fictitious. Novelists, composers, and other creative individuals often imagine alternate worlds.

Imagine for a moment that you have been given the magical ability to live in a world other than your own. People and objects are given new abilities; perhaps gravity is absent. This area is inhabited by both human and non-human beings. We don't know if space exists in other universes. It is possible that the shortest path between two points is not a straight line. Do you think it's possible?

If you can imagine a place like this, then it is indeed a reality. When it comes to virtual worlds, imagination is the starting point. We have the power of imagination to live wherever, whenever, and with whomever we want. We are only constrained by our imaginations and the words we can use to describe them.

It's often necessary to put our thoughts into a tangible form. We are able to participate in other people's creations and share our own with them when we do this. We can travel to exotic locations and experience a different way of life through books, films, radio, television, and animation. However, only one way of communication is produced by each of these media: from the creator to the audience. The viewpoint has already been decided upon. The dialogue is already written. The outcome of the story has already been decided on. However, each audience member is likely to react in a unique way, even if the creator didn't expect it.

Mimesis, a term for how realistic or at least consistent a world is, can determine if a novel is an alternate world that immerses the reader or just a novel that tells a story. Listeners, moviegoers, and TV viewers alike have probably found themselves empathizing with fictional characters at some point. These media appear to be real because of your ability to suspend disbelief. There are, however, no methods that allow viewers or listeners to interact directly with the world. Even more so, these media frequently depict their worlds from a third-person perspective (POV).

Physical immersion, rather than mental immersion, is the first step in virtual reality. Many other media fall within the parameters of our simple definition of virtual reality because physical immersion is a necessary component.

Physical and Mental Immersion

There are two types of immersion: mental and physical (or sensory). We've already mentioned this. For the most part, when people talk about "being immersed," they're talking about the way it feels to be emotionally or mentally absorbed into the story. We use the term "physical immersion" interchangeably with "replacement" or "enhancement" of the participant's senses in VR.

As a result of being fully immersed in one's surroundings, the term "sense of presence" is frequently used. Because there is still a lack of clarity on the meanings, relationships, and distinctions between these terms, it is difficult to use them effectively. As we begin this chapter, let's take a look at what these three terms mean and how they're used in context.

- Virtual reality is defined by its ability to immerse the user in a virtual world, while the goal of most media creators is to immerse the viewer in a virtual world through mental immersion.
- To be mentally immersed means to suspend disbelief and to be fully engaged in whatever it is that you are doing.
- This does not imply that the entire body is immersed or engulfed in the medium, nor does it imply that all of the body's senses are stimulated.

To describe these phenomena, we'll use the terms mental and physical immersion. However, the VR community has also adopted the term "presence" to describe this concept (perhaps because of the prior use of the term telepresence). Our intended meaning might be better expressed with the term "sense of presence" rather than "presence" alone. To avoid confusion, we'll use the term "mental immersion" to describe this concept.

3. Sensory Feedback

By positioning their body in a certain way, participants can choose their vantage point and influence events in the virtual world, unlike in more traditional media. A media experience that does not include these features is less compelling than one that does. We won't get into the philosophical debate about what reality is, but we will consider that there may be more than what we can see and hear with our unaided senses. Physical reality is the term we use to describe the latter. Our thoughts, dreams, and secondhand experiences in novels, films, radio, and so on are all examples of imagined reality. Diegesis is the term used to describe the process of imagining ourselves in the context of the medium. A medium's diegesis includes places and events that are implied to exist or have occurred but are not explicitly shown. To experience virtual reality, we use less of our own imagination and rely more on the imagination of the content creator, which is why virtual reality is becoming increasingly popular. It is a medium that allows us to experience a simulated reality that is as close as possible to the real thing. Additionally, virtual reality can be used to reduce the dangers of physical reality and to create scenarios that are impossible in the real world.

An essential component of virtual reality is sensory feedback. The VR system provides participants with immediate sensory feedback based on their physical position in the virtual world. Virtual reality environments that exclusively display haptic (touch) experiences do exist, but they are rare. Most feedback is received in the visual sense. As a mediating device, computers with high processing speeds are necessary for obtaining immediate interactive feedback. Tracking a user's movement is necessary for a VR system to use its position as the basis for its sensory output. The participant's head and at least one hand, or an object in hand, are typically tracked by a typical VR system. Most major joints can be tracked by advanced systems. Tracking in virtual reality can be accomplished using a variety of technologies.

Computerized sensing of the physical world's position (location and orientation) is a good definition of position tracking.

4. Interactivity

VR must be interactive in order to be convincingly convincing as a genuine experience. As a result, interactivity is an essential part of any comprehensive definition of virtual reality. With the addition of a computer, interactivity is more easily achieved. It is possible to create alternate realities through the use of computers in a variety of contexts.

These alternate realities do not necessitate the use of computer graphics. Classic computer games such as The Oregon Trail, Adventure and Zork (originally known as Dungeon) use only text to describe their environments. As the player types in command, the worlds respond to their commands, making the player feel like they're a part of them. In these imaginary worlds, the player interacts with objects, characters, and places.

Interactive fiction is a term now used to describe the medium of authored, text-based interactive worlds (IF). One example of interactivity is the ability to influence a computer-based world. The ability to alter one's point of view within a world is another variation on this theme. It is possible to define interactive fiction as a form of storytelling in which the player is able to manipulate the world around them by moving around, picking up and placing objects, and so on. Virtual reality is more closely associated with the participant's ability to move physically within the world, gaining a new perspective by moving the head. IF and VR may be defined by a single type of interaction, but both mediums can utilize the other type of interaction.

As true as it may be, much virtual reality (VR) experiences are built with static worlds that cannot be modified by the user. Computational simulations are used to create artificial realities that represent a subset of the real world. As a result of these models, a large number of numerical values representing the state of the world over time can be generated. This could be done by using current weather conditions to solve mathematical equations that describe a thunderstorm and then translating these equations into visual representations of the storm.

Collaborative Environment

Multi-user interaction within a single virtual space or simulation is what we mean when we talk about a collaborative environment. Users are able to interact with each other in the simulation because they can see each other. A user's avatar is a representation of themselves.

For many VR applications, including those in combat simulation/practice and the VR game industry, this is a critical feature that allows for team play and human opponents. Other participants increase the difficulty of a situation by being unpredictable. Other VR applications will benefit from it as well. Because of the convenience of virtual prototyping, designers located all over the world can communicate and collaborate virtually. Multiple surgeons can watch an operation from the same vantage point while using telepresence surgery, and in some cases, they can transfer control to another participating surgeon.

There are times when it is critical to know where the other people in the room are, how they are looking/pointing, and their words when engaging in a shared experience. User representation in a virtual world is denoted by the Hindi word avatar (which means the worldly manifestation of a deity). A person's live video image can be used as part of or the entire avatar representation in some cases.

It's not just virtual reality that allows for multi-presence; it's also possible to experience the phenomenon in non-VR contexts. Because there are two or more participants in a telephone call, it would also be considered a multi-presence virtual environment. As a result of this phenomenon, the term "cyberspace" was coined.

Combining the Elements

Taking into account all of these components yields a more accurate definition:

- Using interactive computer simulations that track the participant's position and actions and provide feedback to one or more senses instead of traditional sensory feedback, virtual reality creates the illusion of being physically present in the simulation (a virtual world).

Using this definition, practitioners of virtual reality will be able to distinguish between the many different types of devices that are used in the medium.

In modern computer systems, additional hardware devices can be used to provide user position sensing, sensory display, and programming of appropriate interaction to meet the scenarios described in the definition Helmets, also known as head-mounted displays (HMDs), may or may not allow users to see what's going on around them.

Depending on the model, the helmet may have a single screen or two screens (one for each eye). The computer system can tell where a participant is looking thanks to a tracking sensor attached to their head. The computer displays a visual representation of the participant's location in a matter of seconds. As a result, the participant can explore a computer-generated world in a way that is as natural and intuitive as possible, given the limitations of current technology. It is possible to incorporate additional devices into such a system so that participants are able to interact with the world in a variety of ways. Voice recognition and a glove connected to the computer allow them to interact with the world through the voice and movement of objects in the world.

Creating a virtual reality experience can be done in a variety of ways, including placing the user in a virtual reality room surrounded by computer-generated imagery. Typically, this is done by projecting computer graphics onto large stationary screens via a rear-screen projection method. As an example, the CAVE system from the University of Illinois at Chicago's Electronic Visualization Lab [Cruz-Neria et al. 1992] is well-known. Even if the participant is only partially immersed in the visuals, the experience can still be engrossing.

Virtual reality (VR) isn't always a visual experience. A surgeon could use computer-connected medical instruments to interact with a virtual patient.

Devices that provide haptic feedback (resistance and pressure) for the doctor's hands, simulating the feel of instruments on the organs, track the doctor's hands.

Artificial Reality

Artificial reality is another term for interactive environments in which a user can participate. The term "artificial reality" was coined by Myron Krueger to describe his research, and it is now commonly known as "virtual reality." A great deal of the material in his second book, Artificial Reality II, is devoted to the topic of artificial reality's relationship to both art and technology. In Krueger's glossary, he defines artificial reality as follows (and I'll quote):

- In an artificial reality, the body's relationship to a graphic world is interpreted as a participant's action and generated responses that maintain the illusion that his or her actions are taking place within that world.

Virtual

THE WORD "VIRTUAL" is often used to imply that virtual reality technology is involved because of the hype surrounding virtual reality. The term "virtual" doesn't imply that it's a virtual reality, but that doesn't mean it is.

A computer system's name can include the word "virtual" to indicate that some of the system's components are extensions of the hardware, emulating the real thing through a different source. Another application is in computer-generated virtual worlds, where objects appear to be real. The word "virtual" can be added to each object's name to indicate that it is merely an image of the physical object it represents. In a virtual world, we can describe a virtual table and a virtual kitchen. Similar to its use in virtual reality, the term "virtual image" is used in the field of optics to describe objects that appear to exist through a lens or mirror.

Virtual World

Virtual environments and virtual worlds are two terms that are frequently misunderstood. What is the relationship between virtual reality and the virtual world? Both "virtual reality" and "virtual world" are often referred to as "virtual environment." However, the term "virtual environment" has been around for a long time. It is possible to define a virtual environment as either a virtual world or a virtual reality hardware configuration. To describe their work in creating an interface that allowed a first-person perspective on a computer-generated scene, researchers at NASA's Ames Research Lab used the term virtual environment in the mid-1980s.

Cyberspace

The term "cyberspace" is also important to understand in relation to these terms. People have been able to communicate with each other via technology (such as the telephone) for many years now. As a result, a brand-new location in cyberspace was born. William Gibson first used the term "cyberspace" in his novel Neuromancer in 1984 to describe the vast network of computers in the future that would allow its inhabitants to search for, retrieve, and communicate data.

Virtual reality is not the same as cyberspace. While virtual reality can be used to communicate in cyberspace, it isn't necessary. There are numerous examples of simple text, voice, or video triggering the creation of a virtual world on the internet. There are numerous other examples of places that can only be found online, such as live chat forums, MUDs, newsgroups, and so on. The telephone, CB radio, and video conferencing are all examples of non-internet communication.

It's interesting to note that this new space is often treated as if it were a real-world place. Here and there, people's use of the words "here and there" stands out. If you want to know if someone is participating in a live chat forum, you might ask, "Is Beaker here?" This refers to the virtual space created by the forum. Even in television interviews where the host says, "Here with us now is an expert in virtual reality, Dr. Honeydew," this same phenomenon occurs. However, that person is frequently not present in their studio at all but rather on a large television screen in another location.

Augmented Reality

In some cases, virtual reality applications are designed to combine virtual representations with real-world perception. Additional information about the real world can be gained by using virtual representations. The term "augmented reality" is used to describe this type of application (AR). Special display technology is used in

AR to allow users to overlay additional information on top of the real world. This word comes from the definition of augment in the New International Dictionary of the English Language (1989): "to increase in size or extent." With augmented reality, we're giving users access to more data than they'd get from their normal senses.

Virtual reality, like augmented reality, can be thought of as a subset of the former. Instead of being immersed in physical reality, one is transported into a hybrid reality that combines the real and the virtual. In most cases, the sense of sight is heightened. Contractors who need information about a building's mechanical systems might display the location of pipe and ductwork on the computer-connected goggles they wear as they walk around the building. In the future, doctors may use AR to examine a patient's internal organs while maintaining a view of the patient's entire body.

Potential AR applications are centered around the idea of repairing living or mechanical systems' internal components. One way augmented reality might be used in medicine is to show doctors and patients exactly where cancerous tissue is located in their bodies. AR could also be used to inform a surgeon where to make an incision in the event of an emergency. A medical student might benefit from a third application if it explains how to properly make an incision.

A mobile visual display is typically required for augmented reality, especially if the user intends to move around in the enhanced world. Head-mounted displays are the most common, but a palm-based display is possible as well. The virtual overlay must be perfectly aligned to the real world onto which it is mapped in order for AR to work. Registration is the term for this process.

Telepresence

Virtual reality (VR) technology is used in telepresence. Transducers such as video cameras and microphones serve as a substitute for the participant's own senses in telepresence. From a first-person perspective, the participant can see and hear in a remote location thanks to remote sensing devices. The user can interact and influence the remote environment through their actions. In contrast to most forms of virtual reality, telepresence depicts the real world rather than one created entirely by computers.

VR technology can be used to place the user somewhere else in space, such as in an adjoining room or a neighboring planet. Telepresence is an application. The fact that so many VR practitioners use the term "presence" is probably due to the fact that telepresence was already a well-established term in the closely related field of remote control operations before VR. The word tele means "far away," while "present" refers to the state of being "here." Telepresence can be used to manipulate deep-sea probes, handle hazardous chemicals, and control spacecraft operations.

Telepresence can be used to solve large-scale issues. Using minimally invasive techniques, a doctor can perform an operation while being observed by a small video camera implanted inside the patient's body. The doctor uses tools that translate the doctor's movements outside the patient's body into relatively small cutting and sewing operations inside the patient's body.

You can interact with a physically real, remote environment from your first-person point of view; there are no restrictions on the remote environment's location, and there are no restrictions on the size of the device used to carry out your commands. First-person telepresence

The term "telepresence" refers to a situation in which the user is able to see the remote world through the lens of a remote device. As opposed to remote control operation, teleoperation involves the use of a remote device by the operator while viewing the remote device through an external camera to interact with the environment.

It is distinct from television, where the participant only observes and does not participate. As a result, teleoperation's requirement for seeing the world "live" (i.e., synchronously) is not met. In general, telepresence is thought of as providing an insider's perspective on the world, whereas teleoperation is thought of as offering an outsider's perspective.

A model airplane can be used to demonstrate the difference between telepresence and teleoperation. It's possible to experience your surroundings virtually through telepresence, but it's much more difficult to do so from a first-person point of view than it is to do so via simple remote (tele) operation. If you're piloting a radio-controlled plane, you'll typically be standing on the ground, watching the plane execute the command you sent it from outside the vehicle. Inside the craft, an onboard camera must be installed so that the user can see what it would look like from a pilot's perspective.

VIRTUAL REALITY, TELEPRESENCE, AUGMENTED REALITY, AND CYBERSPACE

Computer-mediated interfaces to the real and virtual worlds are frequently conflated in terms of the types of interfaces. The terms virtual reality, augmented reality, telepresence and cyberspace have all been defined, but it is worthwhile to take a closer look at the similarities and differences between these closely related expressions.

Virtual reality's cousins augmented reality and telepresence can be compared to each other. The physical world is combined with digitally generated information in augmented reality. The user can interact and influence the remote environment through their actions. We can see and interact with the real world in augmented reality (proximal). Telepresence allows you to see what's happening in the physical world (distal). In contrast to virtual reality, telepresence uses input from the real world rather than a computer-generated one.

Cyberspace and virtual reality have a more nuanced relationship. Their distinguishing characteristics appear to cross over into one another. Unlike in the real world, there is no direct sensory substitution in cyberspace. When a person interacts with a virtual world rather than with other people in the real world, it does not always fall under our definition of "cyberspace" (which may not include other people).

Virtual worlds and communities are both examples of technology-mediated interactions. To be in cyberspace is to be in constant contact with other people's minds. Immersive sensory immersion in a computer-created virtual world constitutes virtual reality. Although cyberspace isn't a distinct medium, it is a feature of many media. The term "cyberspace" refers to the existence of a virtual world in which multiple people (the "we") can interact and be fully immersed.

CHAPTER 5
METAVERSE AND VIRTUAL REALITY

We've seen glimpses of virtual worlds where people can take on any identity they want in many works of science fiction. One of the most intriguing aspects of modern technology is the concept of a virtual world in which you can escape from the real world. You've probably been hearing a lot lately about the latest metaverse developments. However, because of the strong ties between the metaverse and virtual reality, there has been a lot of discussion about the differences between the two.

People who are unfamiliar with the metaverse assume that it is a virtual world that can be accessed through virtual reality headsets. Is virtual reality the same as metaverse? No. There's a lot to tell the metaverse apart from virtual reality. In this chapter, you'll learn how to tell the difference between the metaverse and virtual reality.

THE HYPE BETWEEN METAVERSE AND VIRTUAL REALITY

After major corporations began investing in the metaverse, it became one of the most talked-about topics in the tech industry. Big companies like Facebook and Microsoft are launching their own platforms into the metaverse to compete with the likes of Google and Sony. Only after Facebook's October 2021 announcement of its rebranding as Meta did the term "metaverse" begin to gain traction. What motivated Facebook to take this action?

Intriguingly, the company's announcement that it has sold 10 million Oculus VR headsets marks an important milestone in the debate between virtual reality and the metaverse. Using the internet in virtual environments is a common metaphor used to describe the metaverse. Virtual reality, on the other hand, would only be one part of an interconnected metaverse. For the sake of clarity, let's learn more about the metaverse and virtual reality.

THE METAVERSE

In a metaverse vs. virtual reality debate, you need a thorough understanding of both concepts. In 1992, a sci-fi novelist, Neal Stephenson, coined the term "metaverse" in his novel "Snow Crash." Stephenson describes the metaverse as a virtual world from which the protagonist could escape the real world in his novel.

The main character entered the metaverse as a new avatar, one that was utterly unlike his previous persona. Many of today's definitions of the metaverse are based on Stephenson's original concept. The metaverse is often referred to as the next step in the evolution of the internet.

In a metaverse, users can explore and interact with a variety of virtual spaces, content, and services in three-dimensional environments. There is a creator economy being established in the metaverse as a result of the ability it gives different users to create virtual spaces and solutions.

Many different technologies, including virtual reality (VR) and augmented reality (AR) goggles, allow users to enter the metaverse. The metaverse can also be accessed through a computer or smartphone. Hence, you can see the answer to the question of "what's different between the metaverse and virtual reality" from the clarity that VR is not a part of the metaverse.

Aren't Virtual Worlds Supposed to Be the Metaverse?

Surely, you'd wonder if there are any significant differences between the metaverse and virtual reality. The metaverse is more than just a collection of interconnected virtual worlds. But rather than being a replacement for the real world, it will be an extension of it. The answer to this question can be found in a deeper examination of how the concept of metaverse differs from today's internet.

In the metaverse, you'd be more than just a machine that requests information from web servers. Avatars allow Metaverse users to interact with online content and virtual spaces as if they were in the flesh. As a virtual avatar, users can participate in a variety of experiences in the metaverse. In reality, the metaverse would be a massive, shared virtual world where no one has any restrictions. It's possible to visit a virtual museum in the metaverse without leaving a game.

VIRTUAL REALITY

VR, as the name implies, refers to the creation of virtual environments that are powered by technology. A computer-generated three-dimensional environment is what is meant by the term "virtual reality." In an immersive and engaging environment, an individual could explore and interact with the virtual reality experience.

Virtual reality environments immerse the user and allow them to interact with objects and complete tasks. Virtual reality's definition clearly blurs the line between the metaverse and virtual reality. As a matter of fact, VR can only provide access to walled experiences or limited virtual worlds.

Virtual reality (VR) experiences can be accessed through the use of special headsets and glasses that are linked to the system that is running the programs. Sight and sound are two examples of sensory elements that can be enhanced by using specialized devices.

In addition, there are VR systems that allow users to wear electronic sensors in their gloves. Virtual reality's primary uses have been identified in the realm of entertainment thus far. Virtual reality's applications in education, medicine, and the military are also gaining traction recently.

THE DIFFERENCE BETWEEN METAVERSE AND VIRTUAL REALITY

The basic outline for defining a virtual reality vs. metaverse comparison is provided by the detailed overview of the metaverse and virtual reality. Virtual reality (VR) is a common topic of conversation when talking about the metaverse. The comparisons between the metaverse and virtual reality can therefore be difficult to pass through. Both of them, on the other hand, are vastly different from one another. Listed here are some key differences between virtual reality and metaverse.

Definition

In a metaverse vs. VR debate, the most obvious point of comparison would be their respective definitions. 3D virtual spaces, solutions and environments created by users are accessible in the metaverse, an open, shared and persistent virtual world. VR, on the other hand, uses computer-generated imagery to create three-dimensional simulations that can be customized to serve a narrow range of purposes.

The metaverse, on the other hand, has yet to be precisely defined. As a result, in the virtual reality vs. metaverse debate, VR holds a definitional advantage. The lack of a definition for the metaverse may be puzzling, given that we can see one right in front of us.

There are several ways to conceptualize the metaverse in this context. It is possible to define the metaverse as an embodied internet or a digital world that is open to all, shared, and persistent. You can only find vague descriptions of the metaverse in comparison with virtual reality.

Ownership

Possibilities for ownership are unquestionably the next major difference between the metaverse and virtual reality. A VR system is essentially a brand-owned system that you are experiencing. The content used in the virtual reality experiences on the system belongs to the brand. The only thing you can control with virtual reality is the technology itself.

It's a whole new ballgame altogether when Metaverse lets you own your own virtual assets and experiences. Whether it's virtual real estate or an artifact, everything you create and own in the metaverse belongs to you. Users in the metaverse have full ownership privileges.

Technologies

Discussions about metaverse vs. virtual reality also tend to focus on technological limitations. Virtual reality has certain limitations when viewed from the perspective of the user. Virtual experiences can only get better with the advancements in VR technology. Virtual reality will ultimately be about playing games and having fun in a virtual world.

The metaverse, on the other hand, has no such restrictions. Virtual reality is only one part of the metaverse's power source. Many other technologies, such as augmented reality (AR), blockchain, cryptocurrency, and connectivity, are powering the metaverse's functionality. For the most part, it is a massive virtual world that can be integrated with new technologies to provide enhanced capabilities.

Experiences

In a metaverse vs. VR discussion, the way you experience VR and the metaverse are also important factors to consider. Virtual reality (VR) allows you to feel like you're wearing a headset or other device that allows you to interact with the virtual world. Because of this, only a limited number of people can participate in virtual reality experiences at the same time.

By combining the technologies of AR and VR, the metaverse creates a virtual world that closely resembles the real world. As a result, moving around in virtual worlds feels exactly like moving around in the real world. The most important aspect of the metaverse is that the experiences are not restricted to a single location. Unlike virtual reality, players in the metaverse can visit, experience, and connect with other metaverse users and different metaverse environments.

Persistence

In order to distinguish between the metaverse and virtual reality, persistence is the next factor to consider. In a virtual reality vs. metaverse comparison, VR systems are clearly one of the favorites. While the metaverse is still in development, you can already experience virtual worlds thanks to VR technology. Virtual reality (VR) systems, on the other hand, stop providing experiences the moment you turn them off.

Virtual reality's script is turned on its head when it comes to persistence because the metaverse is a shared and ever-present universe. This means that even if you were to leave the metaverse, your digital avatar would remain. When there are other users in the metaverse, it will run normally.

Shared Virtual World

Users will be able to connect to the metaverse, a shared virtual space, over the internet. Again, this is something that virtual reality headsets clearly already permit. The sound of the metaverse's virtual space is eerily similar to that of virtual reality programs. They expect to be recognized in virtual environments by avatars with which they can interact. Users will be able to buy or build NFTs, for example. Metaverse, on the other hand, sounds like it will have access to the entire internet, unlike existing virtual worlds.

The Metaverse Will Be Accessible in Virtual Reality

The metaverse does not necessitate the use of virtual reality headsets. Most of the services will, at the very least, be accessible for headset users. Thus, it's possible that the line between online activity and fully immersing oneself in a virtual world will blur. Wearable VR devices will soon be used to perform tasks currently done on smartphones. It's possible that VR will become less of a niche product if Facebook's metaverse becomes as popular as they expect.

The Metaverse will not be confined to virtual reality technology.

Continuing from the previous point, the metaverse will not be restricted to a purely digital environment. Instead, it will be available via augmented reality devices as well as any other internet-connected gadgets you already own. This paves the way for a slew of new capabilities not otherwise accessible through virtual reality. In the future, technologies such as augmented reality will make it possible to bring metaverse elements into the physical world. In addition, virtual spaces will be created to be accessed from any location without the use of a headset.

The Metaverse Is Potentially Much Bigger Than VR

Education, therapy, and sports are all examples of how virtual reality is being used. However, it is still regarded as the most popular form of entertainment in the world. In terms of scale, the metaverse sounds a lot like a better and more advanced version of the internet. Virtual reality has been ignored by many people, but the metaverse is expected to have a profound impact on the way people interact with the world around them.

Potential and applications

In comparison to virtual reality, the metaverse appears to have a wider range of potential uses. Virtual reality is now being used in a variety of industries, including sports education and rehabilitation. People, however, continue to view it as a form of amusement. Contrary to popular belief, Metaverse's application potential is much greater. It is, in fact, a better version of the current internet than we currently have. It also has the potential to change the way people work, browse the internet, and interact with social media. In addition, while many people have yet to adopt virtual reality, this appears unlikely in the case of Metaverse.

HOW METAVERSE WILL USE VR, AR AND MR IN NEW WAYS

It's important to remember that virtual reality products are single-purpose investments in which the owners' money is put to good use. There may be an opportunity to open-source the mechanisms of collaboration and interoperability, allowing those experiences to interact with each other and build new, richer experiences than we can currently achieve. It's possible that human-computer interfaces, such as virtual reality, augmented reality, mixed reality, and others, could be used to create a new level of digital life if they can successfully engage content creators in diverse creative communities. Also, it isn't going to be a place where only techies and gamers hang out.

You'll be able to do the same things you're currently able to do with video and graphics in the metaverse. Virtual meetings, multiplayer games, and conference calls are just a few examples. It's also possible that other, less obvious applications will benefit from these new technologies and that this could lead millions of people to purchase XR devices.

Here are a few of the possibilities:

Digital Twins or Mirror Worlds

When a physical object or space is digitally recreated, it is known as a "digital twin" (e.g., through the use of IoT sensors). You may not be aware of it, but you're already using one - Google Maps is a simplified digital twin of most of the world.

So that we can experience the real metaverse through virtual reality technology on VR headsets or even just on smartphones, we will need to create a digital twin—a mirror world for us to move around in. It could be like Minecraft's recreations of real-world landmarks. Engineers and scientists have used nVidia's Omniverse to create 3D digital twins that are stunningly realistic.

We'll be able to visit places and people on the other side of the world from the comfort of our own homes, no matter how it's done. It will also be possible for engineers and architects to simulate threats, planned construction visualizations, traffic and other conditions in the real world. Possibly even in real-time.

However, keep in mind that these digital twins are not yet metaverse, even if they are realistic and fully immersive thanks to virtual reality or mixed reality gear.

Virtual training and procedures in augmented reality

Engineers, medical students and doctors, city planners, and climate scientists are just a few examples of professionals who use XR technology in their work today. Companies are increasingly turning to Virtual Reality and Augmented Reality to train their employees remotely, whether it's workplace safety training, electric grid maintenance, or open-heart surgery.

Virtual real estate and city development

Some investors believe that as the real estate market in the physical world becomes increasingly out of reach for the average person, we will take our house-building fantasies to the metaverse. There are no physical limits to the number of materials or space we can use in a digital world, which is a significant advantage over the physical one. We could spend hours in perfectly designed virtual cities, shopping, working, and hanging out with friends in the metaverse if the right regulations were put in place.

Social life in Virtual Reality

Many people have been persuaded to try online socializing, usually through video chats, due to the rise in social distancing over the last two years. To provide the illusion of a shared virtual space, virtual events and virtual office platforms have evolved and innovated over time. These solutions relied heavily on 2D venue plans and the click of a few buttons on a website.

In the future, we'll be able to feel like we're in the same room as someone we're conversing with or watching on stage, thanks to

Extended Reality technology. Virtual concerts have already taken place in Fortnite and Decentraland. You might soon be able to teleport to a virtual concert or museum with friends on other continents while still attending a concert or to go for a walk in your own neighborhood.

REMEMBER: Virtual reality is well-understood, but the Metaverse is still a mystery. Because the Metaverse appears to be connected to the internet, the difference between virtual worlds and the Metaverse is critical. The Metaverse is an open virtual world where anyone can enter, experience, and interact, in contrast to most VR environments, which are usually restricted to a small number of users. There are no boundaries to the internet's vastness. It's only a matter of time before virtual reality (VR) becomes synonymous with gaming. As a broader concept, the Metaverse is meant to encompass all of the various ways in which people will be interacting with virtual reality in the future. Virtual reality has the potential to fundamentally alter the way we live, work, and interact with the internet.

The Metaverse will be open to anyone, regardless of whether or not they have a VR headset. Using augmented reality devices, for example, it is possible to enter these virtual worlds and project them into the real world. In the Metaverse, augmented reality (AR), virtual reality (VR), blockchain, and social media concepts are used to create virtual environments that mimic the real world. As a result of the merging of augmented reality and the internet, the Metaverse is a collective communal virtual space made up of all virtual worlds and augmented realities.

CHAPTER 6
AUGMENTED REALITY AND VIRTUAL REALITY

What images come to mind when you think of "the technology of the future?" As technology continues to evolve, how will it impact your life in ten years' time? Some people imagine self-driving electric cars that can be summoned at the command of a single word. Others may envision an AI utopia in which robots perform the menial labor tasks that humans have had to do in the past, freeing people up to tackle life's more difficult problems.

People may also envision a time when they will be able to design their own realities. Putting on a headset allows them to experience the atmosphere of a soccer stadium thousands of miles away, even if they're sitting in their own living room. Wearing a pair of high-tech glasses, they could chat with their friend in the form of a fully-realized holographic avatar. They may even imagine an entire room where they could step in and dial up an environment simulation as if they were actually there. Virtual reality (VR) and augmented reality (AR) are technologies that the average person may not have had the opportunity to experience yet, but nearly everyone can envision them as a part of humanity's future. There's a reason for that. In movies, TV shows, and books, we've been sold on the promise of virtual reality for a long time—the VR OASIS of Ready Player One, the VR real-world simulations of

The Matrix, the full-blown environmental recreation of the holodeck from Star Trek. It's not just magic and imagination that's being explored in entertainment these days.

As far as VR and AR concepts go, they're out there. You can wear a headset and be anywhere in the world from the comfort of your home. Whoever you are, you can do anything. It is possible to watch live sporting events or concerts from the comfort of your home. You can jump from planet to planet in a matter of seconds, traversing the entire solar system. In the past, the public has been promised these kinds of virtual and augmented reality (VR/AR). However, this promise has so far failed to live up to the hype.

In recent years, however, computing and manufacturing technologies have caught up with the promises of virtual reality and augmented reality (VR). Science fiction has been brought into the real world. When it comes to new technology, Arthur C. Clarke once stated, "Any sufficiently advanced technology is indistinguishable from magic." While it's possible to use an iPhone in medieval times, it would be considered a magical picture box if it was shown to a person in the past. First-time users of high-end consumer VR headsets frequently describe the experience as "magical."

Virtual and augmented reality (VR and AR) will have a profound impact on our lives within the next decade. As a result of these innovations, our society's course will be drastically altered. But in order to do so, they require the assistance of creators — dreamers, innovators, and magicians.

Before diving into the nitty-gritty of virtual reality and augmented reality, you need a basic understanding of these technologies. As you read through this chapter, you'll learn how to distinguish between various forms of virtual reality (VR) and augmented reality (AR). Also included in this chapter is a quick look back at how we got to this point in technological history. Finally, it discusses the Gartner Hype Cycle, a model for predicting the growth and change of emerging technologies like virtual reality (VR) and augmented reality (AR).

VIRTUAL REALITY AND AUGMENTED REALITY

Many different immersive experiences are referred to as "virtual reality," including augmented reality, mixed reality, and extended reality. The term "virtual reality," as used in this chapter, refers to a computer-generated simulation of reality that creates an artificial physical environment. Typical virtual reality environments are isolated from the real world in that they are constructed entirely from scratch. There is no physical connection between the digital worlds and the places they are based on, such as the summit of Mount Everest or the underwater city of Atlantis.

Viewing the real world while "augmenting" it with computer-generated input such as still images, audio, or video is known as augmented reality, and it can be achieved in two ways: either directly or via a device like a camera that creates a visual of the real world. In contrast to virtual reality, augmentation (adding to) rather than creation (creation from scratch) is the hallmark of augmented reality.

The computer-generated content in AR is an overlay on top of the real-world content, according to the strict definition. Neither of the environments can communicate or respond to the other in any way. A more blended hybrid known as mixed reality, which combines elements of the real world and digital content, has been co-opted in recent years by the AR community.

The term "augmented reality" refers to both augmented reality and mixed reality in this chapter. Both terms are often used interchangeably in the industry, and mixed reality is quickly becoming a more descriptive term for the combination of analog and digital realities. Likewise,

OTHER TYPES OF VIRTUAL AND AUGMENTED REALITY

For now, it's hard to tell which terms will become obsolete and which ones will gain traction in the coming year due to the fact that VR and AR are still at an early stage (s). While the terms "virtual reality" and "augmented reality" are here to stay, there is a slew of new terms to learn about.

Mixed reality

You may be able to interact with computer-generated content in your view of the real world using mixed reality (MR). An alternative is for the system to link real-world objects to a purely digital environment. As a result, MR can at times function like virtual reality and at other times function like augmented reality. When using AR-based MR, the digital world's content can interact with the real world as if it were an actual part of it. Some digital objects can even be interacted with as if they were actually present in the physical world. You might be able to watch a digital rocket take off from your coffee table or bounce a virtual soccer ball off the real-world walls and floor.

In reality, Apple's ARKit and Google's ARCore fall somewhere between AR and MR and reveal the naming discrepancy taking place in the AR and MR industry. However, despite the fact that they project a digital layer on top of the real world, they are also capable of scanning and tracking surfaces in the real world. Using this technology, users can physically place digital objects in the real world, cast digital shadows on real-world objects, and adjust digital lighting to match the lighting conditions in the real world.

An AR-based MR headset like the Microsoft HoloLens scans the real world and then adds digital objects to the mix. In comparison to Apple and Google's current tablet offerings, this technology, which can also be found in Microsoft's Meta 2, goes a step further. Through the use of transparent visors, the virtual environment is projected onto the user's eyes, and their hands can interact with it as if it were real.

However, in other instances of MR, you may only see an entirely digital environment with no view of the real world, but this digital environment is connected to the real-world objects around you. Tables and chairs from the real world may appear as rocks or trees in your virtual world. In the real world, moss-covered cave walls can be seen on office walls. Virtual reality-based MR, or augmented virtuality, is what we're looking at here.

While MR allows for interaction with the digital world, the strict definition of AR does not allow for it. The industry, on the other hand, is blurring the lines between these two extremes. The term "augmented reality" is often used interchangeably with "mixed reality." Their significance will most likely evolve and grow as time passes. Unless otherwise stated, I use AR and MR interchangeably in this book.

Augmented virtuality

Augmented virtuality (AV), also known as merged reality, is a term that has yet to gain much traction in the industry. It is basically the inverse of typical AR. Although the term "augmented reality" (AR) typically refers to digital objects being integrated into real-world settings, "augmented reality" (AV) refers to digital objects being integrated into real-world settings. Video streaming from the real world and placing that video in a virtual space are examples of AV, as is creating a 3D digital representation of an existing physical object.

Extended reality

There is an umbrella term for all of the technologies we've discussed thus far: extended reality (XR) (including VR, AR, and AV). It is possible to measure a technology's level of virtuality or realness using a continuum. The completely virtual is at one end of the spectrum, while the completely real is at the other. XR covers the entire range of this scale.

Virtual reality and augmented reality, two terms that encompass a wide range of emerging technologies, are the primary focus of this chapter. Most situations can be summed up in those two words. My definition of virtual reality includes any hardware/software combination that creates a primarily or entirely digital experience for users to engage in. Any real-world environment that has been enhanced by digital elements is referred to as augmented reality (which may or may not interact with the real environment).

A BRIEF HISTORY

American science fiction writer Stanley G. Weinbaum wrote a short story called "Pygmalion's Spectacles" in 1935 about an inventor who created goggles that allowed the wearer to trigger "a movie that gives one sight and sound, taste, smell and touch." This is your story; you can interact with the characters and hear their responses; the story revolves around you, and you are a part of it." Computers and television weren't even invented when Weinbaum started writing. Weinbaum would probably be shocked if he traveled back in time and saw how closely his vision of VR resembles the current state of emerging technology.

Virtual reality and augmented reality have a rich and diverse history that goes far beyond the scope of this article. In the meantime, a general look at some of the various incarnations of these technologies may provide some clues as to where these technologies are headed in the near future.

The father of virtual reality

According to VR pioneer Morton Heilig, who is widely recognized as the father of virtual reality cinema, a multisensory movie theater called "The Cinema of the Future" was first conceived in 1955. Heilig created a mechanical arcade cabinet called the Sensorama, for which he made a number of short films to engage the senses. Virtual reality headsets of today have a stereoscopic 3D display, stereo speakers, and haptic feedback through vibrations in the user's chair.

Heilig patented the Telesphere Mask, the first-ever head-mounted display (HMD), shortly after developing the Sensorama, which provided stereo 3D visuals and stereo sound. The Sensorama's bulky seated form factor is more akin to today's consumer VR headsets than this (relatively) small HMD.

Augmented reality gets a name

For each aircraft built-in 1990, Boeing Computer Services Research was asked to create a replacement for Boeing's current system of wiring instructions on plywood boards. Construction workers could use a head-mounted display that projected the position of cables onto multipurpose, reusable boards, as proposed by Caudell and his co-worker David Mizell. Wiring instructions could instead be worn by the workers themselves instead of on separate boards for each aircraft. The term augmented reality was coined by Caudell and Mizell.

Early virtual reality failures

During the Consumer Electronics Show in 1993, Sega announced its Sega VR headset for Sega Genesis, a massively popular videogame console at the time (CES). In the fall of 1993, Sega originally planned to deliver the device for $200, a reasonable price at the time. The system, however, was dogged by development issues and never made available to the general public. To Tom Kalinske, Sega's CEO at the time, the Sega VR was put on hold due to testers developing severe headaches and motion sickness.

One of the gaming industry's most well-known names decided to get in on the action, as well. Nintendo's Virtual Boy was the first portable 3D-capable device to be released. It was Nintendo's hope that by encouraging game development outside of the traditional 2D screen space, the Virtual Boy would establish the company as an innovator. However, the Virtual Boy was also plagued by development issues.

Nintendo decided to stick with the red LEDs in the Virtual Boy because the company's initial tests with color LCDs resulted in "jumpy" images. In addition, the Virtual Boy began as a tracking head-mounted system. A tabletop version was developed because of concerns about motion sickness in children, as well as the risk of developing a lazy eye. Critics slammed it. In the year it was on the market, it failed to meet its sales goals and was quickly discontinued. For decades, VR advancements were relegated to research labs and academia due to these early failures and other failed attempts to create mass-market VR devices.

Virtual reality breaks through

AFTER BECOMING dissatisfied with the available VR head-mounted displays in 2010, Palmer Luckey, a tech entrepreneur, set out to create his own. A poor end-user experience was caused by the devices' high cost, large weight, narrow field of view, and high latency, all of which combined to make them prohibitively expensive and cumbersome.

It was a reaction to this frustration that led Luckey to build a series of prototype HMDs, each of which was designed to be inexpensive, low-latency, expansive, and comfortably weighted. Rift Development Kit 1, which he offered on the crowdsourcing website Kickstarter as his sixth-generation device, was called Oculus Rift (DK1). Almost 980 percent of the original goal was met in the Kickstarter campaign, which raised $2.4 million. It's also worth noting that the Kickstarter campaign helped to stoke consumer excitement about virtual reality to previously unheard levels.

Augmented reality hits the mainstream

AR was given a boost in popularity by a surprising source: the smartphone. A few decades after its inception, AR remained in the shadows, much like virtual reality (VR). With the rise of virtual reality in recent years, interest had risen slightly, but nothing was available for mass consumption, and it was not clear when anything would be available.

Apple and Google both released their own versions of AR for their various handheld mobile devices running either iOS or Android in 2017, which gave the technology its biggest boost in public awareness since its inception. Estimates put the number of ARKit and ARCore-capable devices in the hands of more than a quarter of a billion people by the end of 2017.

AR, which had been working in relative obscurity, suddenly had an enormous market of consumers to create content for, and developers began racing to create content for that market. Apps that translate foreign language signs by pointing a mobile device camera at them are just a few examples of augmented reality (AR) applications that can be used for a variety of purposes, including gaming, interior design, and navigation.

EVALUATING THE TECHNOLOGY HYPE CYCLE

Similarly, technological waves experience peaks and troughs before they are adopted by the general public. The Gartner Hype Cycle, a representation of how expectations around transformative technologies play out upon their release, was proposed by the information technology research firm Gartner. When a technology is first introduced, the Gartner Hype Cycle can help predict how quickly it will be adopted (or not). Pre-2007, the markets for the Internet (following the dot-com crash) and mobile phones experienced similar (if not identical) ups and downs.

Early proofs of concept and media attention serve as an Innovation Trigger in the early stages of a technology's development.

The next peak is the peak of overestimation. As a result of the early successes and positive publicity, businesses have higher hopes for the technology than it is capable of delivering. The Trough of Disillusionment that follows occurs when actual implementations of the technology fall short of the high expectations set by the initial Innovation Trigger and media buzz. There are many technologies that fail in the Trough of Disillusionment and never live up to their initial promise.

After weathering the Trough of Disillusionment, second- and third-generation products begin to appear, and the technology and its uses are better understood; those technologies reach the

Slope of Enlightenment. Early adopters who are able to see through the trough with their ideas and executions intact often reap the benefits of mainstream adoption.

Eventually, we arrive at the Plateau of Productivity, where companies that have weathered the turbulence of the hype cycle can reap the benefits of their early adoption. You can make better decisions about VR and AR by knowing where they are in the cycle. Consider whether or not now is the right time for your company to begin implementing these new technologies. Is everything ready to go, or should you wait a few more years before launching?

VR, according to Gartner, will reach mass adoption in two to five years, having just emerged from the "Trough of Disillusionment," according to Gartner. The adoption of AR, on the other hand, is conservatively estimated by Gartner to be five to ten years away due to AR currently being in the Trough of Disillusionment.

It may sound like an ominous place, but the Trough of Disillusionment is a necessary phase for technology to pass through. Before it reaches the hands of consumers, new technology must undergo a rigorous process of establishing its identity and determining its place in the world. Manufacturers must determine which issues it effectively resolves and which issues it fails to resolve effectively. That can take a lot of trial and error to discover.

Adolescence is a good time for AR as a mass-market consumer product. It takes time for manufacturers and developers to figure out what form factor it should exist in, what problems it can solve, and how it can best solve them. Manufacturers of any emerging technology, including virtual reality and augmented reality, should be wary of rushing a product to market before these questions have been answered, as this can often lead to more problems than it solves. This Hype Cycle report for virtual and augmented reality was released by Gartner less than a month after

Apple's ARKit announcement and a full month before Google's ARCore was announced. ARKit and ARCore's release could be argued to have sparked mainstream adoption by virtue of their large installed base. That, however, seems a tad dishonest. Simply having a base installed does not guarantee widespread adoption (though it is a large piece of the puzzle).

When using technology is as easy as opening your web browser, checking your email on your mobile device, or sending a text message to a friend, it has truly entered the mainstream and is no longer a novelty. Only time will tell if either technology can achieve this level of ubiquity. Virtual reality and augmented reality, like the personal computer and the Internet, have the potential to revolutionize our lives in the long term.

As soon as you can get your hands on virtual reality or augmented reality devices, or if you want to start creating content for these technologies, now is the time to do so.

CHAPTER 7
EXPLORING THE CURRENT STATE OF VIRTUAL REALITY

Being a part of VR development at a time when technology is constantly evolving is both exciting and frenetic. It's critical to pause and assess where things stand right now. Within the next year or two, are we on a collision course with the peak of the fourth wave of technological change? In other words, is the current VR cycle just another misstep in the development cycle of virtual reality?

Are we about to enter another decade of virtual reality wallowing in the "Trough of Disillusionment?" after a promising rise and subsequent washout that leaves companies high and dry? Many industry insiders predict that virtual reality (VR) will become widely used by the years 2021 to 2023. Many of the issues that exist today will be resolved by then, as VR headsets will likely be in their third or fourth generation of technology.

This section examines the current technological landscape (as of this writing). Many devices of the first generation have been released, and many devices of the second generation (or first and a half-generation) have been announced as well. Realizing where VR now helps you make your own predictions about the future of technology, allowing you to assess where we are in the VR cycle on your own

THE AVAILABLE FORM FACTORS OF VIRTUAL REALITY

Although there are a number of different types of virtual reality headsets, they all appear to share the same basic design. VR experiences may indeed benefit from this form factor, but it could also be a sign of a lack of innovation in mass consumer devices if there is not more variety in hardware implementations. VR's form factor may change completely in the future. For the time being, the majority of VR systems are implemented as head-mounted displays, but each company has developed its own design for how that form factor should appear and function.

The book's main focus is on the consumer head-mounted displays (HMDs) with the largest user base in order to keep the book's focus manageable and concise. Oculus Rift, HTC Vive, Windows Mixed Reality, Samsung Gear VR, PlayStation VR, Google Daydream and Cardboard are the only ones on the market at the time of writing. At the moment, these are the most widely available first-generation consumer VR headsets, but that may change in the future. Many of the evaluation criteria I include here are likely to be shared by any new headset that comes along. The same criteria can be applied to many of the upcoming second-generation devices. You'll be able to evaluate any new hardware that comes out if you're familiar with the various options, benefits, and drawbacks of different hardware implementations.

HTC Vive and Oculus Rift are currently at the top of our VR experience graph for consumers. It is without a doubt that they provide some of the most immersive virtual reality experiences to date. The headsets themselves, as well as the separate hardware needed to power them, aren't free.

In the same league as the Vive and the Rift, Microsoft's Windows Mixed Reality VR headsets are now available. However, don't be fooled by the name. Microsoft's virtual reality headsets are referred to as "Mixed Reality" in the company's marketing, but there is nothing "mixed reality" about them at this time. Will a pass-through camera image of the surrounding environment allow the products to function as both a VR headset and an augmented reality (AR) headset in the future?

Microsoft may want to go in that direction, but the capability isn't fully present in the headsets it has available right now. However, Microsoft's Mixed Reality platform includes specifications that hardware manufacturers can use to create their own Windows Mixed Reality Headsets, so it's not a specific piece of hardware itself. Similarly, Google Cardboard, which is discussed later in this chapter, works in a similar way. (The HTC Vive and Oculus Rift could be compared to Apple in the sense that each manufacturer creates and markets its own headset hardware and controls all aspects of the product.

Microsoft, on the other hand, only has control over the Windows Mixed Reality software specifications; it is not required to create its own hardware. As long as they adhere to Microsoft's guidelines, third-party manufacturers are free to design and market their own Windows Mixed Reality headsets. Microsoft HoloLens, the company's augmented reality headset, is technically part of the Windows Mixed Reality platform as well. It's possible to get lost in the shuffle. When I talk about Windows Mixed Reality in this section, I'm generally referring to the company's line of immersive virtual reality headsets. The Microsoft HoloLens is one of the devices I frequently refer to when discussing the topic at hand.

It's difficult to make apples-to-apples comparisons when evaluating Windows Mixed Reality VR headsets when there isn't a single standard to use. Microsoft Windows Mixed Reality headsets may have different baseline specifications than, for example, HP Windows Mixed Reality headsets. As a result, most Windows Mixed Reality VR headsets tend to be on the upper end of the VR spectrum.

The PlayStation VR is a video game console manufacturer's take on virtual reality. In order to use PlayStation VR, you do not need a PC, but you do need a PlayStation gaming console. It's easy to use, affordable and has a wide selection of games, but reviewers have taken issue with the lack of a room-scale experience, the underpowered controllers, and the lower resolution per eye compared to higher-end headsets.

To say that one experience is better than the other isn't necessarily the case. Both have their own unique set of advantages and disadvantages. Externally powered "desktop" VR experiences are a good option if you want the most powerful or immersive VR experience possible. The mobile VR headsets may be a better fit for you if image fidelity isn't as important to you and you need to be able to move around while wearing your headset. It's important to keep in mind that this is only an evaluation of the first generation of VR devices. High-end devices will be released in the next year or two that do away with the need for external hardware power or at the very least do away with the wires from experience in the second generation. It will be a huge step forward in making virtual reality more widely available if users can disconnect from their machines in this way.

THE FEATURES OF VIRTUAL REALITY

In addition to price and headset design, each manufacturer is taking a variety of approaches to the VR experience it provides. Some of the most important VR features are discussed in the following sections.

Room-scale versus stationary experience

With room-scale, a user's real-world movements are tracked into the virtual environment, allowing him or her to roam freely around the play area of a VR experience. In order to track the user's movement in three-dimensional space, first-generation VR headsets will need external sensors or cameras in addition to the headset. Is there a school of fish you'd like to get a closer look at? Run after your robot dog on the floor of your virtual spaceship? What better way to learn about Michelangelo's David than to walk around in a 3D replica of it? You can do these things in a room-scale experience if your real-world physical space allows you to.

Virtual reality devices that use inside-out tracking are rapidly replacing older models that require external devices to provide a full-room experience. In contrast, a stationary experience is exactly what it sounds like: a VR experience designed to keep the user seated or standing for the majority of the experience. Room-scale VR experiences are currently only possible with high-end VR headsets (such as the Vive, Rift, or WinMR headsets), not mobile-based headsets.

Users can feel more immersed in room-scale virtual reality experiences because their physical movements are reflected in the virtual world. Walking across a virtual room is as simple as walking across a real one. When she needs to get something from under a table, she simply squats down and reaches under. Using a joystick or similar hardware to accomplish the same thing in a stationary experience would detract from the experience and make it less immersive. Virtual reality (VR) experiences that allow for physical movement go a long way toward making the experience feel more "real."

The disadvantages of working at room-scale are numerous. If you want to be able to walk around in virtual reality without running into physical obstacles, you'll need a lot of open floor space for a room-scale experience. Most of us can't afford to dedicate entire rooms of our homes to virtual reality setups, but developers can use a variety of tricks to get around this limitation.

Real-world physical barriers that prevent users from running into doors and walls must be included in room-scale digital experiences, as must boundaries that show where the physical-world boundaries exist.

Many room-scale VR experiences also necessitate users to travel greater distances than their physical space can handle. In most cases, a straightforward option exists for those who wish to travel while remaining seated. All of her stationary experiences must either take place in a single location or use a different method for moving around since she can't physically move around during them (for example, using a controller to move a character in a video game). It's a different set of issues when it comes to room-scale experiences. A user can now move around in the virtual world, but only to the extent permitted by the user's unique physical configuration.

In virtual reality, some users may be able to walk as far as 20 feet. It's possible that other users' physical VR play areas are constrained, with only 7 feet of emulated walking space. VR developers must now make some difficult decisions about how to allow users to move around in both the physical and virtual environments. They must choose between several different approaches. Is there a solution if the user needs to get to a part of the room that is just a tad outside the usable physical space? Do you want to go around the corner? or even miles away?

In room-scale virtual reality, a user may be able to simply walk across the room to pick up an object. In the case of long-distance travel on a room-scale, however, complications arise. Whenever a user can physically move closer or further away from an object, developers must decide whether or not to allow the user to do so. The solutions to these issues exist, but because virtual reality is still in its infancy, the best practices for VR developers are still being experimented with.

Inside-out tracking

At this time, only high-end consumer headsets can provide realistic room-scale simulations. A wired connection to a computer is usually required for these high-end headsets. Users are forced to step over the wires as they move around the room. Wiring is required for both the display of images in the headset and for the tracking of the headset in the real world.

In the second generation of virtual reality headsets, manufacturers are looking for ways to eliminate the need for a wired display. Streaming video to a headset without a wired connection is being researched by companies such as DisplayLink and TPCast in the meantime.

Outside-in tracking systems for the Vive and the Rift are currently constrained by the fact that the headsets and controllers are tracked by an external device. Outside of the headset, additional hardware is placed around the room where the user will move around while in VR space (called sensors or lighthouses for Rift and Vive, respectively). Unlike the headset, these sensors are not part of it. In 3D space, their placement around the room allows for extremely accurate tracking of the user's headset and controller, but users are restricted to movement within the sensor's view. Tracking is lost when the user leaves that area.

With inside-out tracking, there is no need for external tracking sensors because they are built into the headset. In order to coordinate the user's movement in virtual reality, the headset must interpret depth and acceleration cues from the real-world environment. Inside-out tracking is currently used by Windows Mixed Reality headsets.

A "holy grail" for virtual reality, inside-out tracking removes the need for external sensors, allowing the user to roam freely. However, it has a price, just like any other technological decision. Internal tracking is currently less accurate and suffers from other drawbacks, such as losing track of controllers if they travel too far out of the headset's field of vision. Second-generation headsets, on the other hand, use inside-out tracking to improve physical movement in virtual reality. Even with inside-out tracking, defining a virtual reality "playable" space may still be necessary. You'll still need a way to tell where you can and can't go in the area. Inside-out tracking is a big leap forward for the next generation of virtual reality headsets because it eliminates the need for external sensors.

First-generation VR headsets still require a computer or external sensors to operate, but companies are finding creative ways to overcome these limitations. The VOID, for example, has implemented its own innovative solutions that provide a glimpse of what a fully self-contained VR headset could offer in terms of experience. They call it "hyper-reality," and it allows people to interact with digital elements in a physical way.

The VOID's backpack VR system is the company's technological lynchpin. By mapping out entire warehouses of physical space and overlaying them with an exact digital representation of the physical space, the VOID is able to create a one-to-one digital representation of the physical space. Numerous new options now become available as a result of this. The VOID can create a digital door dripping with slime and vines in place of a plain real-world door. In the digital world, what might appear to be a bland gray box can be transformed into an evocative oil lamp that guides the user through unfamiliar territory.

The VOID's current backpack design is unlikely to succeed on a mass consumer scale. It's cumbersome, expensive, and probably too complex for a large audience. This isn't necessarily a bad thing, as it provides a taste of what immersive virtual reality could be like if cords and cables were removed. Both the HTC Vive Focus (which is already available in China) and Oculus's upcoming

Santa Cruz developer kits appear to be gearing up to ship wireless headsets as early as 2018.

Haptic feedback

Virtual reality controllers already include haptic feedback, which is the sense of touch designed to convey information to the user. Rumble/vibration can be used to convey contextual information to users of Xbox One, HTC Vive Wands, and Oculus Touch controllers. You're about to grab something. You're putting your finger on a switch. You've shut a door behind you. But the feedback these controllers offer is rather limited. " Using these devices, you get the same sensation as if your phone vibrates when you get a notification.

If the industry wants to make virtual reality feels as real as the real world while inside it, haptics must be taken a step further than it has so far been. Touch in virtual reality is a problem that many companies are trying to solve.

Go Touch VR has created a VR touch system that can be worn on one or more fingers in order to simulate physical touch in virtual reality (VR). In essence, the Go Touch VR is nothing more than a pressure pad that you wear on the tips of your fingers. As the company *Go Touch VR* claims, users will have the sensation of holding onto an actual object in the virtual world. Some other companies, such as Tactical Haptics, are attempting to fix the controller's haptic feedback issue. They claim to be able to simulate the types of friction forces you'd feel when interacting with physical objects by using sliding plates in the surface handle of their Reactive Grip controller. It is common to feel your tennis racquet push against your hand when making a swing.

You'll feel more resistance against your hand when moving heavy objects than when moving light ones. To paint by hand, you'd feel the brush drag against your hand as if it were being dragged across paper or canvas. These scenarios, according to Tactical Haptics, can be accurately simulated in a way that most current controllers cannot. Companies like HaptX and bHaptics are developing full-blown haptic gloves, vests and exoskeletons for virtual reality. The wireless TactSuit is currently being developed by BHaptics. A haptic mask, vest, and sleeves are all included in the TactSuit. It uses eccentric rotating mass vibration motors to disperse the vibrations across the wearer's face, vest front and back, and sleeves, all while retaining the wearer's full range of motion. With this technology, bHaptics claims that users can "feel" explosions and weapon recoils as well as being punched in the chest through their virtual reality headsets.

With its HaptX platform, HaptX is one of the companies experimenting with haptics in virtual reality to the fullest extent. With the help of HaptX's smart textiles, you will be able to perceive the texture, temperature, and form of objects in your environment. At the moment, it's working on a haptic glove prototype to give virtual reality (VR) users realistic touch and force feedback. HaptX, on the other hand, goes a step further than most haptic hardware's standard vibrating points. Microfluidic air channels embedded in the textile push against a user's skin, allowing for force feedback that can be transmitted to the wearer.

When compared to other haptic devices, HaptX claims that its use of technology provides a far superior experience. If combined with virtual reality, HaptX's system takes users a step closer to immersive virtual reality experiences. HaptX's system could lead to a full-body haptic platform, allowing you to truly experience virtual reality.

Audio

In order to replicate reality as closely as possible, virtual reality (VR) must use other senses besides sight and touch. 3D audio, on the other hand, is ready to take the world by storm. A realistic experience relies heavily on involving the user's sense of hearing; in order to give the user a sense of presence and space, audio and visual elements work together.

Along with visual cues, it is possible to use audio cues to guide users through an online experience. A sound's 3D direction of arrival, general distance to the source, and so on are all discernible to the human ear. An audio experience must be replicated in order for a user to feel as if she's actually listening to it in the real world. It has been possible to create a 3D audio simulation for some time, but this was usually done as a quick fix. 3D audio has found a market that can help it advance with the rise of VR (and vice versa).

A wide range of current headsets, including Google Cardboard, can play spatial audio. Listeners who have their ears on opposite sides of their heads can benefit from spatial audio. The user's left ear will receive sounds from the right side of the device with a delay (because the sound wave travels slower to the ear farther away from the audio source). It used to be that before spatial audio, apps would simply play sounds from the left or right speaker, cross-fading between them.

Stereo recordings are made with two microphones spaced apart, recording two separate channels of audio. To create a loose sense of space, the sound can be panned between each channel in this method of recording. Use of microphones that simulate a human head produces two-channel recordings known as binaural recordings. Playback through headphones can be extremely lifelike, thanks to this. Binaural recordings of live audio in virtual reality can provide a very immersive experience for the end-user.

Both spatial and binaural have one drawback: Headphones are required to experience 3D effects. This isn't a deal-breaker for most VR headsets, but it's something to keep in mind when comparing headsets.

VIRTUAL CONTROLLERS

If you don't have a system of input that is as high-fidelity as the visuals, your virtual experience will quickly lose its potency. When a user moves their hands or feet in a virtual world, the immersion is shattered because those movements are not reflected in the virtual world. Oculus Rift founder Palmer Luckey told The Verge, "The virtual reality experience will not be complete with just the visual side." In order to interact with the virtual world, you must have a fully integrated input/output system that allows for both a natural view and a natural interaction.

As you explore the world of virtual reality, you'll come across a variety of input devices and features. These range from the simple to the complex. They all have different ideas about how virtual interaction should work. The simplest input solution, such as a gaze to trigger an action, may sometimes be the best solution for the experience. In some cases, nothing enhances the immersion experience more than a fully-realized digital hand mimicking the movements of a user's real hand.

Toggle button

Toggle buttons are so commonplace that they don't even need to be listed here. In addition, the Google Cardboard is currently the only virtual reality headset with a built-in controller. (As of this writing, based solely on the number of devices sold.)) When it comes to buttons, there isn't much to explain beyond pointing them out where they are (or pointing them in the right direction if they don't know where they are). Actions begin when you press the button.

Integrated hardware touchpad

A touchpad built into the side of some headsets, like the Gear VR from Samsung, takes the concept of an integrated hardware button a step further. Using a touchpad instead of a toggle button provides a better user experience. The touchpad allows the user to swipe horizontally or vertically, tap on items, toggle volume, and exit content as necessary. Additionally, the touchpad serves as a replacement for a device's motion controller if the user loses it.

One drawback of integrated control solutions is that they must be able to communicate with the device that is actually running the experience. For example, some mobile VR headsets with built-in hardware controls may require a micro-USB (or similar) connection to the mobile device. Touchpads also have the potential to pull users out of the virtual world because of their lack of natural integration with it (i.e., they don't simulate the controller in the virtual world).

Gaze controls

Virtual reality applications can incorporate gaze controls into their user interfaces. If you're looking for a more passive VR experience, these are a great option for you. For example, instead of using a touchpad or motion controller, you can simply stare at the control for a predetermined amount of time to activate it. Gestural controls are frequently used for less active applications, such as video and photo viewers, where the user is more passively engaged.

Furthermore, the use of gaze controls is not limited to passive interaction. In VR, the gaze is frequently used in conjunction with other methods of interaction (such as hardware buttons or controllers). The use of gaze controls is likely to increase in popularity as eye-tracking becomes more widely accepted. Controls for the user's gaze include a reticle (or cursor), a timer, and other features. A few seconds of focused attention is all it takes for the user to select or initiate an action on a given item. In addition, gaze controls can be used in conjunction with other types of input for deeper interactions.

Reticle is any graphic used to show where the user is looking in virtual reality. When using headsets that don't have eye-tracking, this is typically where a user's eyes are trained. The reticle, which is often just a simple dot or crosshair, sits on top of all other elements to help the user visualize what they're currently picking. In the interim, until more advanced eye tracking in headsets becomes widely available, a reticle in the center of view can provide a simple solution.

Keyboard and mouse

Interacting with a VR headset can sometimes be accomplished through the use of a standard mouse and keyboard. When using a headset, it's difficult to see the keyboard, which can be a drawback of this setup. Even the most proficient touch-typists find it difficult to type if they are unable to look down at the keyboard, even for a brief moment. Using a mouse, on the other hand, has its drawbacks. The mouse has long been the primary means of navigating in 2D digital environments, such as on desktop computers. However, in a 3D environment, the user's gaze should be controlled by the headset. It was possible to change a user's perspective using both the mouse and their physical gaze in some early applications, but this interaction could be extremely confusing because the mouse would pull a user's view in one direction while their physical gaze would pull it in a different.

Some VR apps still support keyboards and mice, but those input methods have largely been replaced by more integrated solutions. These new integrated solutions, on the other hand, may have their own drawbacks. Long-form text can no longer be entered into applications using a keyboard as the primary input device.

For this issue, a variety of solutions have been proposed. Logitech has developed a virtual keyboard for the HTC Vive that allows users to see a virtual representation of its keyboard. To help touch-typists around the world, Logitech has created a 3D model of its keyboard in your virtual reality space right on top of the physical version of the keyboard.

There are also text input methods that are completely digital. Predictive typing is made possible by Jonathan Ravasz's Punch Keyboard, which uses motion controllers as drumsticks. A better method of text input is needed if VR applications are to gain widespread consumer acceptance.

Standard gamepads

For many gamers, a familiar input method is the standard gamepad (or videogame controller). Many gamers were already familiar with the Xbox One controller when the original Oculus Rift was shipped.

The problem with gamepads in VR is that they don't feel as integrated with other input options. It was a good first step away from keyboard and mouse, but for many VR users who are also gamers, they were familiar. Rather than using standard gamepads, most VR headsets now appear to prefer more integrated motion controllers as the primary input method. Lack of digital integration was the primary problem with standard gamepads. The user can be yanked out of the VR experience by the difference in the physical and digital experiences of using the gamepad. As a result, the majority of headsets have developed their own motion controllers.

Motion controllers

The de facto standard for VR interaction has quickly shifted from motion controllers, which were once primarily a gimmicky device for 2D PC games. Most major headset manufacturers have released motion controllers that work with their products.

In an ideal world, the end-user would be unable to tell that the controller is even there. Users must make conscious decisions outside of the VR experience when using many of the input methods discussed in this chapter: I am now clicking a button on the side of the headset. As of this moment, I'm scouting the keyboard for the W key. Using motion controllers is a step toward eliminating the problem of input being separate from your virtual reality experience. Virtual reality (VR) often makes motion controllers appear as if they are an extension of the user's hand. Some of the more expensive VR controllers include six degrees of freedom-of-movement capabilities to further enhance immersion.

Movement in three-dimensional space is referred to as having six degrees of freedom (DoF). Orientation tracking (rotation) and position tracking (translation) are two terms used interchangeably in virtual reality to describe the ability to move forward, backward, up, and left/right. 6 degrees of freedom (DoF) enables accurate tracking of the VR controllers in relation to their physical position and rotation.

To keep up with the more expensive models, the first-generation mid-tier mobile headset options (Gear VR and Daydream) have added motion controls as well. The higher-end headsets had more options, but now they've been condensed. It is most commonly implemented as a single controller with various features (a touchpad, volume controls, Back/Home buttons, and so on) integrated into it. Users can see what their hands are doing in the real world by using a digital representation of their controller. These controllers are typically limited to three degrees of freedom, unlike the more advanced motion controllers (only tracking their rotation in the virtual space).

Gear VR and Daydream headsets' controller tracking is impressive for mobile devices, but it falls short of the high-end, tethered headsets'. In addition, the motion control can sometimes feel like a glorified TV remote without a second motion controller (one for each hand). These one-handed control representations, despite being less sophisticated than the higher-end motion control options, can still provide a more integrated VR experience than the previously discussed options. Seeing the controller in the virtual world and tracking its physical movement is a huge step toward immersing the user in virtual reality and incorporating a user's physical movements into the virtual space.

A pair of wireless motion controllers is included with most high-end headsets (such as the Rift, Vive, and Windows Mixed Reality). Overall, the motion controllers have a lot in common with each other despite some minor differences.

Submillimeter object detection is possible with these high-end controller pairs. Another important step in making the VR experience truly immersive is being able to look down and see a visual representation of the controllers moving in tandem with your physical body. Increasingly, virtual reality applications are focusing on motion controllers as their primary input method. For the time being, VR interaction appears to be dominated by motion controls. There are and will continue to be a plethora of other ways to interact in VR.

Hand tracking

Virtual reality headsets can track a user's hands without the need for additional hardware on the user's hands, thanks to hand tracking. Some people believe that hand tracking is the next step in motion controller evolution. This is an avenue being investigated by a number of companies for both VR applications. More and more people are turning to this method of control in AR applications. Hand tracking has been a long-time focus of companies like Leap Motion, both inside and outside of VR. In 2012, Leap Motion released its hand-tracking controller for use with 2D displays. As virtual reality (VR) became more popular, the company saw the potential of its technology for interaction in that space and shifted its focus there.

Hand tracking differs from traditional motion controllers in that it displays a virtual representation of your hand in place of a controller, wand, or other similar virtual "fake" model. In the same way that your physical hand pinches, so does your digital hand. Digital hands respond to the flexing of human hands. Your digital hand makes the same gesture as your physical one. Virtual reality (VR) with full finger tracking allows you to see a digital representation of your real-world hands. Feels like trying on a completely different body. To watch your digital representation open and close its fist in VR, you may have to stare at the hand you're holding.

There are still some issues with hand tracking's visual appeal, however. Virtual space interaction is more limited than it is with motion controllers. Numerous hardware interactions are possible when using a motion controller. The buttons, trackpads, and triggers on the motion controller can all fire off various events in the virtual world. With hand tracking alone, there are no such options. A hand-tracking-based application will have to deal with a wide range of input scenarios. This can be a difficult task, given that only the user's hand is involved.

However, hand tracking can be impressive in its own right, but it lacks the tactile feedback that a user would expect when engaging in real-world interactions. If you're using hand tracking alone to pick up a box in virtual reality, you'll miss out on the sensation of picking up a real-world object.

For the foreseeable future, hand tracking is likely to be a secondary consideration in the design of standard consumer virtual reality (VR) experiences. However, hand tracking will eventually find its way into virtual reality. A once-in-a-lifetime experience like this can't be ignored in the digital world.

Eye-tracking

The first VR headset with built-in eye tracking was released by FOVE in 2016. Each of these companies has acquired eye-tracking startups for use in their various VR and AR devices, indicating that this is a promising area to watch. A user's VR experience could benefit greatly from eye-tracking. Most current headsets (aside from the FOVE) only determine where the user's head is turned, not where the user is actually looking.

Most headsets use a reticle that sits directly in the center of the user's view to informing the user where her gaze is centered, as we discussed earlier in this chapter. The real world, on the other hand, frequently sees people looking in directions other than directly in front of their faces. In spite of the fact that you may be staring at a computer screen directly in front of you, your gaze is frequently drawn to the bottom or top of the screen to select various menus or to your keyboard or mouse.

Adding foveated rendering to applications will be made possible through the use of eye-tracking. In foveated rendering, only the area a user is looking at directly is rendered in high definition, while the rest of the image is rendered at a lower quality. Because current headsets don't "know" where the user's gaze may be, they must render the entire viewable area in full definition at all times. A single area is rendered in full at a time using focused rendering. Complex VR environments can now be rendered on lower-powered computers as a result of this reduction in processing power, making the technology more accessible to everyone.

Developers such as Tobii and 7invensun are focusing on creating foveated rendering hardware that can be added to existing VR consumer devices, despite FOVE's focus on eye tracking in its own headset. Onboard eye-tracking for headsets may be a generation or two away, but it's definitely a development to watch, as most major headset manufacturers have kept quiet about their plans to add eye tracking to their next generation of devices.

THE CURRENT ISSUES WITH VIRTUAL REALITY

A number of technical hurdles remain before consumer-grade virtual reality (VR) can truly reach its mass-market potential, but it is becoming lighter, cheaper, and more polished. With the surge in VR investments that have occurred over the last few years, we should see a quicker turnaround in finding solutions.

In the following section, we'll look at some of the most pressing issues facing virtual reality right now, as well as some of the innovative solutions being developed to address those issues. A case of the dreaded "sim flu" Motion sickness was a common complaint among users of the first generation of virtual reality headsets. Sega VR and Nintendo's Virtual Boy were both doomed to failure due to this issue alone. Manufacturers of modern headsets are still battling this problem.

When your inner ear's vestibular sense of motion is inconsistent with what your eyes are seeing, motion sickness can occur. You may think you are sick if your brain thinks your body is sending inconsistent signals because of some sort of disease or toxin, but this is not necessarily the case. Anxiety and stress can trigger the release of chemicals in your brain that can cause a variety of unpleasant symptoms, including headaches, dizziness, confusion, and nausea. VR headsets can cause a sickness known as "simulation sickness," which is a form of motion sickness that doesn't necessarily involve any real movement.

A variety of approaches, including some that might seem strange, can be used to combat simulator sickness. According to Purdue University's Department of Computer Graphics Technology, a "virtual nose" should be added to all virtual reality applications in order to stabilize the user. Nasum virtual is the name given to this virtual nose by Virtualis LLC for commercialization. Virtual reality sickness can be alleviated by placing the user's nose in their field of view. You can see your nose in the real world, but you may not be aware of it. A 13.5% decrease in sickness severity and a 13% increase in simulator time were reported by Virtualis users, who didn't even notice the virtual nose in VR.

As a VR developer, you can combat simulator sickness by minimizing latency between a user's physical movement and the headset's response. When we move our heads, the world around us responds immediately. There is no lag time. The headset's lack of latency is of the utmost importance here. More than ever, the number of frames per second (FPS) that a headset can display is critical as VR becomes more widely available on low-powered mobile devices. In this way, the headset's visuals can follow the user's every move.

Additionally, when developing or utilizing VR applications, the following tips can help prevent simulator sickness:

- The headset should be properly positioned and adjusted. It's very likely that your headset needs to be adjusted if the virtual world appears hazy while wearing it. Users can adjust the headset's fit and distance from their eyes to remove any blurriness from their video feeds. Before beginning any virtual reality experience, make sure your headset is properly adjusted.
- It's time to get down. Being seated provides a sense of security for some people who suffer from motion sickness.
- Ensure that the content is readable. Keep text usage in VR to a minimum and avoid reading or using small-font text (just a few words at a time).
- As a result, there will be no surprises. Never programmatically move the camera when developing.

The user should be able to tell whether the motion is triggered by his own movement or by interaction.

- Take care when accelerating. Simulator sickness can be avoided by moving virtual cameras in a smooth fashion. Allow the user to move in the virtual world without accelerating or decelerating them.

- Always keep an eye on where the user is going. Don't reverse the camera or stop tracking the user's head position when the user is moving. The view of a user must change as she moves her head.

- Avoid items that can only be viewed from a certain angle. If you're playing a 2D game, you'll see a lot of fixed-view items (e.g., a pop-up notification or a heads-up display [HUD]) in the middle of the screen. However, this mechanic does not work well in virtual reality because it is not something that people are used to in the real world.

Simulator sickness due to low FPS should, in theory, decrease as devices get more powerful. Simulator sickness can be minimized to a greater extent if the user's physical movements are closely tracked by the virtual world's graphics and movement. In spite of the fact that we have surpassed the processing power of computers from decades ago, we still encounter software that runs slower than games from that time period. To a greater or lesser extent, the more power we have, the more we expect from it. Improved graphics! The screen is getting a lot more crowded! Expanded viewing areas! We're getting even more effects now! In order to avoid simulator sickness, you should be aware of the possible causes.

The screen-door effect

Put on an older VR headset or one powered by a smartphone and pay close attention to the image that appears in the headset. You may see "lines" between the displayed pixels depending on the device's resolution. If you sat too close to your old TV set as a kid, you might have noticed the same thing. The term "screen-door effect" refers to this problem's resemblance to looking out a screen door. In some VR headsets, this issue has been reintroduced despite the fact that it has been long solved for modern televisions with extremely high resolutions.

Displays with lower resolution, such as older headsets or some smartphones, show this effect the most prominently because they are held inches from your nose and magnified by optic lenses. Several solutions have been proposed to this issue. A "light diffuser," for example, has been suggested by LG, but most agree that higher-resolution displays are the best solution. The screen-door effect can be alleviated by using high-definition displays, but this will necessitate more processing power. Better hardware, as with simulator sickness, should make this effect less common. Within the next generation or two of virtual reality headsets, the screen-door effect should be a thing of the past.

Movement in VR

It's still difficult to move around in VR's digital environment. For example, the Vive and Rift allow users to be tracked around the room, but not much further. Adding more features requires either a movement mechanic built into the app itself or specialized hardware that is beyond the capabilities of the majority of consumers.

Applications' ability to move across large areas in VR may face logistical challenges in the future. Some users may experience simulator sickness even if they use some of the previously mentioned solutions to move in VR in a way that corresponds to physical motion. Users may not want to walk long distances, even if Omni-directional treadmills could be guaranteed for every user to track their movement. For people with limited mobility, walking long distances may be impossible. Hardware and software developers must work together to find a solution to this problem. Furthermore, options exist.

Health effects

The greatest unknown here is the impact on one's health. Using Oculus Rift while pregnant, elderly, tired, or suffering from heart conditions is discouraged by the company's Health and Safety guidelines. Users may also experience severe dizziness, seizures, or blackouts as a result of using the product. That has a creepy ring to it. Virtual reality's long-term health effects are also unknown. The long-term effects of VR headset use on the eyes and brain have yet to be thoroughly studied by researchers.

Initial studies show that most adverse health effects are temporary and do not have a long-term impact on the user's well-being. The longer-term effects of VR use will necessitate more research as users begin to spend longer periods of time in VR space. Until further notice, virtual reality companies appear to be taking a more cautious approach to long-term effects. VR has the potential to have negative effects, according to Sarah Sharples, the president of the Chartered Institute of Ergonomics and Human Factors, in an interview with The Guardian. The most critical thing we can do is to exercise caution and common sense. We should, however, not allow ourselves to be deterred by this technology's enormous potential."

Cannibalization of the market

The VR market as a whole is also a concern. The mobile market has a massive advantage over the higher-end headsets in terms of adoption. Google Cardboard is the cheapest implementation. Perhaps for a good reason. Buying a $20 low-end mobile VR headset is easier on the wallet than saving up a few hundred dollars for a higher-end headset.

Low-cost headsets, unsurprisingly, provide low-quality experiences. Because they mistakenly believe a low-end VR system is representative of the current state of VR immersion, users may write them off as nothing more than a toy.

Perception, on the other hand, can frequently become a reality. As more low-end VR devices become available, could they hurt virtual reality's overall market share in the long run? The sales figures of lower-end devices may have prompted some companies to pay more attention. As many headset manufacturers appear to be going multi-tiered with their next generation of headsets, they are able to cater to a wide range of consumers. When Oculus co-founder Nate Mitchell spoke to Ars Technica about the company's upcoming three-headset strategy for its next generation of consumer headsets, he said that the Oculus Go, a lower-end standalone device, would be the first, followed by the Oculus Santa Cruz, a middle-tier headset. It is a similar story with HTC. The HTC Vive Pro was released as a high-end device, while the standalone HTC Vive Focus was released in China.

The potential long-term market for virtual reality is likely to be large enough to support a wide range of products. Next-generation headsets have arrived, and we'll be watching to see which devices gain the most traction. Midrange mobile device headsets are expected to grow in popularity in the near future, while high-end, external PC-based headsets are geared toward those who are going all-in on high-end gadgets. Those who fall into the latter category are a more limited market, but they are willing to pay more for the best-in-class experience that virtual reality can provide.

CHAPTER 8
EXPLORING THE CURRENT STATE OF AUGMENTED REALITY

AR has recently experienced a resurgence of sorts. Virtual reality (VR) has a long and distinguished history, and as a result, AR has received less attention from the general public than VR. AR has always seemed to be a distant second to virtual reality in the minds of consumers, whether the concepts were more nebulous to understand or VR was seen as the "sexier" technology.

The years from 2013 to mid-2017 saw the most dramatic increase in this. With the resurgence of virtual reality (VR) headsets, augmented reality (AR) was once again pushed to the sidelines. However, in the fall of 2017, something unexpected occurred. With the introduction of ARKit and ARCore by Apple and Google, the creation of augmented reality (AR) apps for iOS and Android devices has never been simpler for programmers. Due to this announcement, the total number of AR-compatible devices has risen to nearly 500 million (the installed base of compatible iOS and Android devices).

AR-based applications aren't for everyone, but those who want to give it a whirl don't have to shell out for additional hardware.

Like VR, AR appears to be experiencing some of the same problems as the latter at the moment. In the same way that

Google Cardboard helped popularize virtual reality (VR), ARKit and ARCore are boosting consumer awareness of augmented reality (AR). The Meta 2 and Magic Leap are superior in terms of wearable technology, but the HoloLens, HoloLens, and Meta 2 do not provide the same level of immersion. What's most intriguing is where AR's adoption rates are estimated by researchers. Research firm Gartner, using its Technology Hype Cycle, claims that VR has begun its journey down the Slope of Enlightenment and that mass adoption of VR is expected within the next two to five years (2020 to 2023). In the Trough of Disillusionment, it claims AR is currently languishing, with mass adoption expected in five to ten years (2023 to 2028).

You can use the information in this chapter to help you make an informed decision about when AR devices will be widely adopted by the general public. It also outlines some of the hurdles that AR must overcome before it can begin ascending the Slope of Enlightenment for consumer use.

THE AVAILABLE FORM FACTORS OF AUGMENTED REALITY

AR, unlike virtual reality, is still trying to find the best form factor for it. Unlike virtual reality, AR is still trying to find the best form factor for it. AR is available today in a variety of forms, including glasses, headsets, large tablets, mobile phones, projectors, and heads-up displays (HUDs).

There's a good chance that any or all of these devices could be used in AR applications. Alternatively, it's possible that none of these will be the "best" way to experience AR and that another implementation will be released and reign supreme. (Perhaps AR-enabled wearable contacts?). In the meantime, let's take a look at some of the most popular executions currently on the market. Because of the wide range of AR form factors, it's impossible to categorize AR experiences as I did for VR headsets in the previous chapter into high, middle, and low-end options.

In the current AR landscape, each form factor offers a vastly different experience, and each one targets a distinct market. Here, I'll go over the most common form factors, as well as the intended audiences for each of them.

Mobile devices

AR experiences on mobile devices, despite being on the lower end of the spectrum, currently make up the majority of the market for AR. AR has been available in rudimentary form in a number of popular apps for some time now, but many users are unaware of it. A primitive form of augmented reality (AR) on mobile was being used by you every time you added bunny ears to your Snapchat image or saw a Pikachu playing in your local park.

The release of ARKit and ARCore has made it easier for developers to create AR experiences on mobile devices. In order to create AR-based apps for iOS and Android, developers will need to use ARKit or ARCore. Digital holograms can be placed in the user's environment with ease, thanks to features like plane detection and ambient light estimation, which make the holograms appear more real to the end-user. The two products share a similar feature set (which is capable of detecting the ambient light and transferring that information to digital holograms).

There are two software development packages that developers use to write apps for specific hardware: ARkit and ARCore. Both iOS and Android devices can be used with them, but neither is a piece of hardware. Apple's and Google's augmented reality mobile implementations don't require you to buy a separate device; you can use your current mobile device if it meets the ARCore or ARKit minimum technical requirements.

AR headsets

Many AR users begin their journey on their smartphones, but this is by no means the best way to experience the technology. Mobile's physical design can lead to a frustrating user experience. In order to use digital augmentation, a user must constantly hold a device and capture the image of the real world onto which the digital overlay is applied. Another issue is that due to the current form factors of mobile devices, the combined real and digital worlds can only be seen through a very small window (the size of the screen). Virtual reality (VR) applications can benefit greatly from the use of a headset. Microsoft HoloLens, Meta 2, and Magic Leap are just a few examples. This is the first snag we've run into with AR headsets, and it illustrates how far behind VR headsets AR headsets are in the development cycle right now.

Despite the fact that these three headsets are among the most well-known in the field, none of them has yet become a mainstream product. The HoloLens is currently on the market, but it's primarily aimed at businesses and corporations, not individuals. There is a developer kit for the Meta 2, but it has yet to see a full release. As of this writing, the Creator Edition of Magic Leap's headsets has yet to be shipped to developers, despite the company's impressive team and investor group (though Magic Leap announced a ship date of 2018).

A large headband or helmet with a translucent visor attached to the front appears to be the most common form of AR headset. The goggles' surface is projected with images from the headset, creating a digital overlay on the real world. Goggles and light fields make up the form factor of the Magic Leap One, which employs a different approach. HoloLens, for example, is an entirely self-contained headset that allows for more freedom of movement at the cost of a lower processing capacity. Others (such as Meta 2) rely on the processing power of a desktop PC and thus limit your freedom of movement. With its Lightwear goggles powered by a Lightpack (a small wearable computer) attached, it serves as an intermediary between the two.

An interesting addition to this group is the Windows Mixed Reality headset. Microsoft's approach to virtual and augmented reality (VR and AR) suggests that the two technologies will eventually merge. With front-facing cameras instead of a translucent lens, the current Windows Mixed Reality headsets could serve as a pass-through for an augmented reality experience, similar to the HoloLens and Meta 2. However, this feature is not yet available. Currently, the Windows Mixed Reality headsets are only virtual reality devices with no augmented reality capabilities. Only time will tell if Microsoft's naming and positioning of these devices indicate that they will be used for more than just virtual reality headsets.

The current generation of AR headsets provides the best experience currently available, but they are only short-term solutions. In the end, no one knows what the final form factor of AR will be. It could be a headset like Microsoft's Windows Mixed Reality, or it could be a form of AR glasses.

AR glasses

The best way to experience AR in the near future may be through a pair of glasses. Virtual reality glasses have yet to be released in the form of the HoloLens or Meta 2, which are currently more like large visors. However, Magic Leap One is still a rather large pair of goggles. In terms of simple AR glasses, Google Glass and Intel Vaunt are the most well-known examples. Google Glass, on the other hand, is nothing more than a wearable HUD. Digital content can't be "placed" in the real world with its limited resolution and lack of interactivity due to its small viewing area, lack of graphic capabilities, and lack of ability to "place."

HUDs, such as Google Glass, are interesting in their own right, but they are not considered true augmented reality devices. Rumors are rife about Apple's plans to produce its own pair of AR glasses following the release of ARKit and CEO Tim Cook's praise of AR as the future of technology. Apple has yet to make a statement about this. For the time being, the only way to access augmented reality content is through a mobile device or one of the few available augmented reality headsets.

AUGMENTED CONTROLLERS

AR/MR controllers typically face a different set of challenges than VR controllers, and this sets them apart from other types of controllers. As compared to most virtual reality headsets, many AR headsets allow the user to see the real world around them either via video feed or by using a translucent visor. This can alleviate some of the issues that traditional headsets may have. When a user is able to see into the real world, they are no longer fumbling around for real objects.

This improved perspective can also exacerbate other technical issues. Due to the fact that they can see the real world, it can be awkward to interact with digital holograms that are displayed as real-world objects using a controller. This necessitates the development of a system that allows users to interact with digital objects solely through the use of their hands.

It is possible to interact with objects in AR using various methods.

Touch

In mobile AR implementations, touch interaction is most commonly used. AR's use in popular mobile apps like Snapchat has pushed the technology into the mainstream. A few drawbacks have come along with the implementation of augmented reality on non-AR devices (such as smartphones).

The use of mobile device input methods in augmented reality (AR) applications is one of the challenges. Users are familiar with tapping, swiping, and similar actions to the screen on their mobile devices, but these actions may not be sufficient to control and navigate an AR experience.

When it comes to implementing augmented reality on a mobile device, there is no new hardware involved. Instead, they must adapt to how people currently use mobile devices. App developers are usually responsible for deciding how AR input is handled on mobile devices. Users can interact with AR content using a combination of gaze controls (covered in the next section) and standard mobile interactions. If a user positions his/her gaze cursor/reticle over a digital hologram in 3D space, he/she can tap the mobile screen to select it and then drag the digital hologram once selected.

Gaze

IT'S common in AR to use gaze control, just like in virtual reality. While other interactions like gestures or controller clicks may also be used, gaze controls are often used in conjunction with other actions, such as looking around the environment and focusing on a specific object. With mobile gaze controls, it's easy to see where the user's gaze will take a digital hologram in the real world by using a grid that follows their gaze. This hologram of Android's bugdroid mascot is placed on a virtual grid overlaid on top of the actual scene to aid the end-user in visualizing its location.

It's not uncommon for users of headset-based AR applications to see what they're about to interact with via a small reticle (also known as a cursor or crosshair). As a result, applications can determine where a user's attention lies and where it doesn't. Cues can be triggered by an app if it needs a user to focus on an important object in the scene.

The current state of gaze controls in augmented reality is adequate, but when combined with eye tracking, they will be excellent. Virtual and augmented reality (VR and AR) currently require the user to turn his or her entire head in order to look at digital objects. Future eye tracking implementations promise to make this method of selection much more natural-feeling and intuitive to users. As a general rule, when you want to focus on something, you don't typically turn your entire head toward it. You're more likely to focus on items by moving your head and your eyes together. AR headsets will be able to take into account not only the position of the head but also the position of the eyes, thanks to eye-tracking. Expect the use of gaze tracking in AR to skyrocket when eye tracking goes mainstream.

Keyboard and mouse

When we imagine the future, it's easy to imagine a world without keyboards and mice, flying through a completely digital landscape and manipulating our digital environments with futuristic control input methods. A keyboard or mouse may still be the best current method of input for a wide range of tasks. Current AR implementations are aware of this. As an example, the Meta 2 can be used with both a keyboard and a mouse.

The use of a mouse in Meta 2 is anticipated to become obsolete in the future as hand tracking technology improves, but some tasks, such as entering long text, may still benefit from using a keyboard. It's possible, however, that the need for a keyboard for input will diminish as voice control becomes more commonplace.

Voice

Conversing with a machine in a language we understand is one of the most rapidly developing emerging technology fields, as demonstrated by its rapid growth. Conversative UI and artificial intelligence are quickly finding their place in society, from Amazon Alexa to Google Home to Siri. It's only a matter of time before voice and speech become the primary control method for virtual reality and augmented reality. It's easier to learn how to use voice commands than traditional hardware-based controls, which have a much steeper learning curve. Virtual reality (VR) applications can be controlled using voice commands, removing the need for users to learn a new system.

Both Google and Apple have built-in digital assistants in their mobile devices, so Magic Leap has shown off voice control for its AR implementation. As a result, Microsoft's AR headsets, including the HoloLens and Windows Mixed Reality headsets, rely heavily on voice commands.

Standard controls in Microsoft's HoloLens include a set of speech commands that Microsoft hopes will become the norm in AR (such as select, go to start, teleport, go back, and so on). Custom audio input options can be used by developers to create their own voice controls. A dictation option makes it possible for users to enter text into apps without having to deal with the awkward digital keyboard that many VR and AR apps have.

Despite the fact that voice will probably never be the only way to input AR applications, most AR devices are going to have a big role in voice input in the near future.

Hand tracking

As one of the main differences between AR and virtual reality, you can see the world around you in AR. This includes being able to see your hands, which are the most common tools you use to interact with the world around you. In AR, hand tracking is much easier and less problematic than in VR because of this visibility. The core experience of some AR headsets includes gesture input via hand tracking. While most major VR headsets have treated hand tracking as a nice to have but not a necessity, hand tracking is a first-class citizen in AR. Hand tracking for AR headsets and glasses will likely be like the mouse for traditional two-dimensional screens. It is possible to interact with the digital holograms on display in the Meta 2 and HoloLens headsets using standard gestures.

Outside of AR, a company such as ManoMotion is attempting to bring gesture analysis and recognition into this space. It's notable for its support of mobile AR, allowing developers to add this more "natural" method of interaction via gestures to their mobile applications, where a better method of AR input is sorely needed. Manomotion

You may notice that most AR headsets have a problem with tracking your hands when they're outside of your device's or headset's line of sight. This is a major issue. To put it another way, if you want to use gestures, hand motions, and the like, you'll need to bring your hands up to your face. In the real world, it's not a big deal if you're able to get around without using your hands in front of your face. It's important to know how to type, use a mouse or a video-game controller, and so on. In order to track users' hands when they are out of sight, a separate piece of hardware is required, which defeats the purpose of providing friction-free hand tracking in the first place. The ability to track hands outside of the line of sight is expected to improve in the next generation of AR headsets.

Motion controllers

HoloLens Clicker, a device designed to allow users to click and scroll with minimal hand motion as a replacement for the airtap gesture, is one of the simple peripherals included in headsets like Microsoft's HoloLens.

Natural non-hardware controls like voice and gestures and full-blown motion controllers are bridged by simple controllers like the Clicker. For example, users can select a hologram by glancing at it and clicking it, or scroll by clicking and dragging the Clicker and then rotating it to the desired position by pressing the button and holding it. While the Clicker doesn't address all of these issues, it's still an improvement. You don't have to keep your hands within the headset's line of sight to select items when using it casually.

Higher-end devices include Microsoft's motion controllers for its current generation of Mixed Reality headsets or Magic Leap's "Control" controller with six degrees of freedom. AR's motion controllers are likely to be very similar to VR's. Similar to what we've seen with VR motion controllers, we can expect AR motion controllers to try to replicate the natural feel of using our hands and gestures.

For example, using motion controllers in augmented reality (AR) could allow for additional hologram selection and movement options that gestures alone cannot. Compared to VR, there are currently fewer controller options for augmented reality. VR has a leg up on consumer devices, whereas AR has a lot of work to do in terms of hardware. There are, however, some patterns that can be discerned. The goal of augmented reality (AR) is to bring the digital and physical worlds together. Making the connection between the physical environment and digital content as seamless as possible will be the most critical step in the process. Create that frictionless relationship with users by using the least intrusive hardware solutions (such as hand tracking or voice input) and focusing on natural user interaction.

Touch, gaze, voice, and hand tracking are all likely to be used to interact with your AR holograms in the near future.

THE CURRENT ISSUES WITH AUGMENTED REALITY

AR has long been seen as a shadow of virtual reality. The public's imagination has long been captivated by the idea of visiting completely virtual worlds that are distinct from our own. AR, on the other hand, has long been used in business environments, such as manufacturing. As a result, users could become more comfortable with the technology at work, which could lead to an increase in home use of augmented reality for consumers.

Research firm Gartner expects VR to be widely adopted by 2020 to 2023, while AR is predicted to become widespread a few years after that. Accordingly, it may be a decade before we see the widespread adoption of AR that we've all come to expect. Both virtual and augmented reality face technical challenges. There are a lot of similarities between augmented reality (AR) and virtual reality (VR), but there are also a lot of differences, including the need for computer vision to detect real-world objects, the need for transparent displays, the need to place digital objects, the need to fix digital holograms in place in the real world, and many other things.

Form factors and first impressions

AR's biggest challenge may also be one of the biggest hurdles it has to overcome in its battle with virtual reality. Virtual reality (VR) can only be experienced with the purchase of a VR headset and a computer to power it. AR can now be accessed by hundreds of millions of people thanks to the inclusion of AR in standard mobile devices. A less-than-optimal AR encounter, on the other hand. However, despite the efforts of Apple and Google's engineers, most people's first encounters with augmented reality will be limited to the capabilities of a mobile device, despite the efforts of these engineers.

You never get a second chance to make a first impression, as the saying goes. Having a poor mobile AR experience can lead users to dismiss AR as a whole as only having the capabilities of a mobile AR experience to offer in terms of technological advancement. Many other AR-capable form factors may be overlooked in the process. This is a mistake.

Cost and availability

There is no simple answer to the "first impression" problem. Only a few augmented reality (AR) headsets and glasses are currently on the market, and those that are either aimed at businesses or are "developer editions" are not yet ready for the general public. AR headsets and glasses can easily cost thousands of dollars, putting them out of reach of all but the most dedicated early adopters and innovators. This is in contrast to low-cost VR headsets. This discrepancy in price between AR and VR could explain why AR's mass adoption is predicted to be several years away.

As a technology, augmented reality and augmented reality headsets are still in their infancy or the Innovators stage. Getting over the Early Adopters' hump and crossing the divide to reach the Early Majority consumer adoption stage can be difficult for new technologies.

Perceived usefulness

When it comes to computer systems, even the most cutting-edge hardware is worthless without equally impressive software. Many people are intrigued by AR's potential, but they are unsure of what they would do with it. Because popular media has explored virtual reality in relative depth, many people are aware of the advantages it offers. For the most part, however, AR has been kept more of a secret, making it difficult for the general public to imagine how it will be used.

A chicken-and-egg scenario could be at play here. In order to make software for hardware that hasn't yet reached a certain level of usage, developers are reluctant to do so, and consumers are reluctant to buy hardware that doesn't have a wide range of applications for them to use. Buying these gadgets requires a compelling reason.

In order to spur widespread adoption, a few enterprising software developers will need to create a few "must-have" applications. It's not going to be an easy road for these software developers to get their hands on the first "killer" AR applications.

Tracking

The ability to place digital objects in real-world three-dimensional space is a key feature of augmented reality. With the help of a real-world marker, it's possible to indicate where an object should go, but marker-free tracking is the ultimate goal of many augmented reality applications. As opposed to marker-less tracking, which necessitates more sophisticated computer vision, marker-based AR can provide a very stable foundation for tracking. The marker is all that is required.

Computer vision is a term often used when talking about AR. If you're interested in learning more about computer vision and how it can be used in the context of augmented reality (AR), you'll want to read on.

It is technically difficult to develop computer vision that can handle AR without markers because it necessitates a thorough understanding of 3D space in the real world. The difference between what our eyes see and what a computer sees is that our brains can easily distinguish between different types of surfaces, but a computer only sees a collection of pixels, with no one pixel having more significance than the others. How a computer can read a collection of pixels and decipher what they mean is referred to as computer vision. Computer vision, for example, would allow an application to recognize a table image not only as a collection of pixels but also as a 3D object with a height, width, and depth.

Marker-free AR can be slowed down even on systems that can process the necessary data for AR. While some augmented reality devices (such as the HoloLens) are faster than others at processing the environment, many augmented reality devices have tracking latency (delay).

Changing your mobile device's position or shifting your head position quickly enough may cause the digital holograms placed in physical space to shift, even on the best current-generation devices. The real world, on the other hand, would lead you to believe your home was haunted if you saw a chair move or slide across the floor when you turned your back. Much augmented reality (AR) applications still suffer from poor tracking.

AR tracking is one of the most challenging aspects of the technology, but it is essential to maintaining the illusion that a user's digital items are actually present in the real world. You can expect the next generation of gadgets to prioritize and improve upon current-generation tracking technologies.

Field of view

A digital hologram's field of view (FOV) is the area in which it can be seen. FOV (field of view) is a term that refers to the amount of viewable space on your mobile device screen. You can see what's going on in the AR world through your device's screen. The real world, devoid of holograms, is visible only if you turn your gaze away from this portal into the digital realm. In some current AR headsets and glasses, the digital FOV covers only a small portion of the viewable area rather than the entire area of the visor or glasses. It's as if you're peering into a tiny window or letter slot to see the virtual world.

Obviously, a larger field of view is better than a smaller one. Seeing the holograms get cut off within your field of view can easily detract from the overall experience of the game. A 90-degree field of view appears to be the most expansive of the current crop of headsets, but it's still a long way from the human eye's FOV (approximately 135 degrees vertical and 200 degrees horizontal).

With the next generation of hardware, AR is expected to take a big step forward in terms of improving the field of view (FOV). One of the biggest complaints about the HoloLens is that the field of view is so small. Microsoft has already announced that it has found a way to more than double the current FOV in its next generation of HoloLens.

Visuals

Currently, available AR headsets, like current VR headsets, are unable to meet the high-resolution expectations of consumers. Additionally, poor occlusion is a problem with many current augmented reality devices (the effect of an object blocking another object). When we talk about occlusion in AR, we're usually talking about physical objects blocking our view of digital ones. This is a problem in augmented reality mobile apps like Pokémon Go that you may have noticed: Zubat can appear to float above the ground in some scenes, while Squirtle appears to be wedged inside a wall in others. In AR, occlusion is not properly implemented, resulting in these kinds of visuals. It is possible to place digital objects accurately and realistically under, partially behind, on top of, or in any other relation to real-world objects.

Currently, Magic Leap demo videos appear to show a very high level of occlusion (although the device has yet to ship, it is impossible for us to predict whether the production device will be able to meet the high bar set in its video demonstrations).

The top and side legs of a table completely obscure the digital hologram of a robot. Magic Leap's mass-consumer device could take AR to the next level if it can replicate this level of occlusion and fidelity of graphics. When viewed in the context of the marker-less orientation described earlier in the chapter, it may not appear to be much. An understanding of 3D space is required by simulation software if the robot is to be placed behind the table leg. It must be able to view the scene and determine what should be in the foreground, what should be in the background, and how the digital hologram should fit into all of this. Under the table, it needs to know what "forward in space" means and which parts of a table are closer together than others. That's a tall order.

CHAPTER 9
THE FUTURE OF VIRTUAL AND AUGMENTED REALITY

Many of the advances in virtual reality (VR) since the Oculus DK1 Kickstarter in 2013 have been fueled by that initial spark, which has made VR a hot industry. As soon as second-generation hardware goes on sale, momentum from the first generation will have faded, and reality will begin to take hold of virtual reality. Is the first generation's explosive trajectory going to be repeated by the second? Or will the hype fade as early adopters are lured away by a newer technology object? Alternatively, will VR settle into the Slope of Enlightenment, where it slowly gains adoption as more and more applications for the technology are revealed, or will it fall somewhere in the middle?

For better or for worse, VR is going to undergo a lot of changes in the next few years. What you can expect in the market is what I'll tell you about. You may also want to think about how you might be able to get ready for these changes.

THE NEAR-FUTURE CHANGES IN VIRTUAL REALITY

It's the best way to prepare for the future unknown is to review what you already know. It's possible to get a sense of where the market is headed by looking at the second generation of VR headsets, evaluating upcoming trends, reviewing new hardware accessories, and keeping an eye on the more cutting-edge startups.

Evaluating the market

Virtual reality headsets' first-generation adoption rate was a common criticism of the current market. Some people believe that the VR industry has not received a sufficient return on its investment, given the large sums of money and media attention it has received. Virtual reality's critics point to slower consumer adoption rates as a failure. Although this may be a valid criticism, the problem may be more a result of unrealistic expectations than a breakdown in the technology. When it comes to virtual reality, it's easy to get swept up in the hype and expect instant results.

For those in the virtual reality industry, this slower rate of adoption can be discouraging. They're eager to share their work with the world, but first, the world has to catch up to them. For a first-generation device, VR has seen reasonable uptake. Lower-tier devices, on the other hand, have accounted for the majority of those sales. Those devices are fine, but the true transformative power of VR is based on how immersive an experience can be provided. Higher-end (and more expensive) VR headsets typically deliver better-quality (and more immersive) VR experiences than cheaper models.

A chicken-and-egg problem may arise as a result of this. The most immersive VR headsets may become more affordable for the average consumer. There is still a long way to go before content creators can get their hands on the best VR headsets. As a result, this can lead to a self-sustaining feedback loop: As fewer people use high-end devices, there are fewer applications available for them, resulting in a smaller market share for high-end devices. To get out of the loop can be difficult.

It's normal for new technologies to experience setbacks in their development. The awkwardness of adolescence helps to shape well-adjusted people. Even though consumer-grade VR is still in its infancy, it has already shown that it is capable of delivering engaging experiences. User experience appears to be getting better and better with each generation. Now all that remains is for virtual reality to find its niche market. What are the most in-demand attributes? What is the market's maximum tolerance for price? It's more likely, though, that there are multiple markets, each with a different skill set that can be served.

Virtual reality may seem a little strange to think of as a product that is still trying to find its audience. However, millions of first-generation devices have been sold and are still being used on a daily basis. Facebook CEO Mark Zuckerberg wants a billion people to experience virtual reality. Expectations accompany lofty goals. In order to reach such a large audience, VR will need to identify its target market(s).

Looking at upcoming hardware and software

However, what about the next generation of virtual reality software, accessories, and other options for immersive experiences? And how will this impact the consumer??? Virtual reality has spawned a slew of companies devoted to making the experience more immersive, and as headsets have improved, so have the software and accessories that go with them. It's impossible to predict which of the many new industries that virtual reality has spawned will survive and thrive in the long run. Due to their popularity, hardware manufacturers are incorporating third-party features (such as wireless adapters) directly into the next generation of headsets. Although eye-tracking and other features are on the VR headset roadmap for the foreseeable future, most likely, they will still be provided by third-party vendors. Other features, such as the ability to smell in virtual reality, will likely be available only as add-ons from third parties for some time.

Although many of the following features are unlikely to be included in the next generation of headsets, they are expected to make a significant impact in the near future.

Haptics

Sense of touch may be the next frontier for virtual reality, having already established itself in the realms of audio and visual immersion. Companies such as HaptX, GoTouch VR, and UltraHaptics all offer a variety of ways to experience haptics in virtual reality and could point to VR's next big leap in user immersion.

Eye-tracking

Some of the potential benefits of eye-tracking include an increase in the expressiveness of avatars, improved item selection speed and accuracy as well as vastly more efficient graphics via foveated rendering. It's possible that headsets will include eye-tracking in the future, but it's unlikely that most headset manufacturers will do so. It's almost a given that this feature will be included in VR headsets in the next generation or two. The benefits outweigh the drawbacks. The next big step in virtual reality technology will be provided by third-party companies such as Tobii and 7Invensun, for the time being.

Social/communication

While many social apps have been released for VR, social interaction still feels like VR's missing feature. Apps such as Against Gravity's Rec Room are excellent at finding the right balance between a "purely social" app and a game and force its users to engage in social interactions. Rec Room reduces the awkwardness of meeting strangers in virtual reality by forcing users to play games with other users.

Apps like Pluto VR allow users to connect in VR in ways that aren't tied to a specific game. Pluto is able to communicate with other VR users via any VR app. Pluto can turn any VR experience into a place where you can meet new people by running as an overlay on top of your current VR experience. Pluto, on the other hand, isn't considered a social app by its creators. In the words of Pluto VR co-founder Forest Gibson: "We are not a social application. "We see ourselves as a direct communication app," the company says.

You can chat with your friends in Pluto while using any virtual reality app. When you're in a virtual reality environment, they appear as floating avatars to chat. The Pluto avatars of your friends will remain with you regardless of which apps you choose to open.

In the future of virtual reality, social interaction and communication will play a significant role. It's possible that headset manufacturers can come up with ways to encourage this kind of interaction, but they won't be able to solve the issue on their own. The direction of social interaction in virtual reality will have to be determined by software developers.

REMEMBER: Within the next few years, social VR is expected to see a significant increase in popularity. VR software developers will continue to work on social interaction in the near future.

ASSESSING THE FUTURE OF AUGMENTED REALITY

Much of the second generation of virtual reality (VR) devices will be released in 2018 and 2019, but most augmented reality (AR) hardware devices have yet to see their first mass consumer release. To ensure that a market is established before a product is released to the general public, many devices are still released in "developer preview" mode. Additionally, some companies are only accepting preorders for their upcoming augmented reality hardware, which will not be available for purchase until later this year.

No accurate assessment of the potential hardware adoption of AR can be made until larger-scale rollouts, and consumer releases of AR headsets have begun. The manufacturers of AR headsets are likely still experimenting with how to make AR accessible to a wider audience.

The information in this section is based on what we already know about the potential uses of AR. I'm curious to see if the hype surrounding AR is warranted and what that means for the future, as much of AR is still in the "hype" phase. Finally, I touch on what you, as a content creator or a consumer, can expect from augmented reality in the future.

THE NEAR-FUTURE CHANGES IN AUGMENTED REALITY

We can't know what AR will look like in the near future. A wide range of speculative and probable future products exists in the AR market, making it both exciting and frustrating. AR market forecasting is an art as well as a science; it takes some research and guesswork to know what to take seriously and what to disregard.

The AR market can be a difficult one to analyze. It's going to be difficult to sort through all the predictions and promises. Maintaining an eye on the industry and potential new products is always a good idea, but don't get distracted by rumors and speculation. Focusing on currently available hardware and software will allow you to eliminate a great deal of irrelevant information.

Evaluating the market

Future augmented reality applications will most likely fall into two categories: mainstream mobile and enterprise. These are capable of running on a variety of hardware platforms but are most likely to take the form of a headset or eyewear. In addition, most users must get used to a new paradigm with AR. As an example of a new technology that came with a significant learning curve for consumers, consider smartphones. Customers had to adjust to this new form factor slowly over several years. As it was, the transition from a large 2D screen to an even smaller 2D screen was essentially the same thing. Despite the fact that many people had never used a touchscreen device before, they had at least some familiarity with how to use one.

When it comes to interacting with the world around us, AR is an entirely new approach. Consumers would need time to get used to the new way of consuming content even if an inexpensive mass-consumer AR device were released tomorrow. They haven't been able to agree on the best practices or standardized interactions between manufacturers and consumers. For AR, many of the things we take for granted on our computers or mobile devices (click and drag, copy, paste) are still being worked out.

AR headsets for the general public are still a long way off because of the steep learning curve and the lack of consumer hardware and software. It's easy to imagine mass-market adoption of AR headset hardware being at least two to four years away unless a new competitor (such as Google or Apple) enters the fray unexpectedly.

There are encouraging signs that headset AR will be adopted in the future. With the introduction of ARKit and ARCore by Apple and Google, the general public can now experiment with augmented reality for the first time. AR on mobile devices may not be perfect, but this early introduction will go a long way toward starting consumers on the AR learning curve. Mobile devices There will be a much smaller mental barrier to overcome when a mass-market AR headset is introduced.

AR is rapidly gaining traction in the business world, particularly in a few niches. AR could be quickly adopted in the industrial sector. Despite the wide range of industrial applications, many focus on reducing production time and errors. A HoloLens or Meta 2 may be prohibitively expensive for the average consumer right now, but in the context of an industrial setting, even a small increase in worker productivity can quickly pay for itself.

CHAPTER 10
WEB 3.0: HOW WILL IT IMPACT THE FINANCIAL SECTOR?

The Internet is about to undergo a major transformation. Data formats and software that are open will help this revolution along with the exponential growth of artificial intelligence and machine learning, as well as the rapid development of blockchain technology. Greetings from Web 3.0, the third generation of internet services and the next stage in the evolution of the web!

Web 3.0 is believed to add a more intelligent and connected internet. Semantic web technology aims to build a system that can understand and interpret data and knowledge. How we work and collaborate will be transformed by Web 3.0, the upcoming redesign of the web. An IoT (or Internet of Things) rich in data will be born out of this transformation into a dynamic smart web and infrastructure. There will be digital information in this spatial web Executive summary that will blur the boundaries between the virtual and the real world.

The global economic landscape is evolving. In a cashless and virtual economy, FinTech and new-age technologies are firmly entrenched, and Web 3.0 will transform how we work, learn, transact, and interact. For data categorization and storage in Web 3.0, there will be no need for central control points. The safety and storage of this decentralized network will be aided by distributed ledger technologies like blockchain. There will be no barriers to entry or permissions in Web 3.0. With the arrival of Web 3.0, we examine the plethora of opportunities that will be available. Financial services and capital markets will undergo a major transformation in the near future. A new era in technological history will begin, and we will be there to witness it.

MAJOR COMPONENTS OF WEB 3.0

Blockchain Network

Web3's blockchain technology is a key component. Web 3 is built on blockchain technology, and decentralization is at its core. Blockchain technology enables data to be distributed, decentralized, and open. So users can freely trade their data without fear of losing ownership, losing privacy, or relying on intermediaries. In addition, you can log in securely over the Internet without anyone noticing. While Web3 is still in its infancy, blockchain-based tokens and virtual currencies will play an important role. Other than that, users are rewarded for their contributions to the platform's growth by being open about how they monetize and contribute to online improvements.

Artificial Intelligence

Advances in AI have made it possible to make useful predictions and even lifesaving actions that could otherwise have been impossible. Web 2.0 has had its share of AI, but as long as the big tech companies control most of the internet traffic, it remains largely human-driven. Human error and skewed ratings of some internet services, as well as biased product reviews, are unavoidable in the digital age. Most online review services allow customers to leave feedback. It's a shame when businesses hire large groups of people to write stellar reviews of their products or services. People can be paid to give a negative review of an app or service in the opposite direction. Web 3.0's mission is to make it harder for people to perpetrate these kinds of attacks. Because it helps distinguish between legitimate and fraudulent actions, artificial intelligence is an essential component of the internet.

AR and VR

Playing games with others is a common pastime in the metaverse. For this application, virtual reality (VR) and augmented reality (AR) is the primary platforms (AR). The company's blockchain projects are built on fungible tokens, like those used to buy virtual land or avatar outfits. Metaverse is still in its infancy and is still a work in progress. Users and technologists are excited about the potential of the technology, which is still in its infancy.

Many people have high hopes for the future of the metaverse:

- Web3's metaverse technology will be built using blockchain systems and open standards, and it will run on a network of computers around the world rather than a single entity.
- The three technologies of augmented reality, virtual reality, and holographic projections will be used to create Web3 applications.
- To make virtual reality transactions possible, an NFT will be used.
- Access to the metaverse would be unrestricted by the traditional gatekeepers.

CHARACTERISTICS OF WEB 3.0

Listed below are some characteristics of Web 3.0:

Decentralized

No single system has access to all of the Web3 data because it is stored in the blockchain. It's spread across a number of different mediums. Decentralizing access and increasing the likelihood of failure is the result of this.

Permissionless

Web3 does not require any special permissions for users to access the Internet. To use certain services, users will not be required to provide any personal information. Neither privacy nor other information will have to be compromised.

Secure

The decentralization of Web 3.0 makes it harder for hackers to target specific databases in contrast to Web 2.0.

WEB 3.0 AND ITS DEVELOPMENT

The first version of the World Wide Web was called Web 1.0. Most users were content consumers at this point. Web 1.0 was primarily a content delivery network that made it possible for users to access information on other websites. This is what made it special:

- There were no dynamic pages.
- The server's file system was the primary source of content.
- Pages were created by utilizing Server Side Includes or the Common Gateway Interface.
- Frames and Tables were used to position and align elements on a page.

Essential to the development of Web 2.0 is the shift from Web 1.0 in the way digital information is created, distributed, manipulated, and archived. End-users benefit from its user-generated content, ease of use and interoperability. The term "participative social web" refers to a group of internet technologies that will be used in the future. When it comes to how we think of the internet today, we see it as a place where we can interact and collaborate with others. This is how you can describe Web 2.0:

- Web-based applications you can use and access anywhere.
- Straightforward solutions to specific issues.
- Value is placed on the content itself, not on the software that displays it.
- Data that can be easily shared.
- Distribute from the bottom up, not the top down.
- Tools that can be accessed and used independently by customers and employees.
- Sharing and promoting information are encouraged by the use of social media tools.
- The more people who contribute, the better the content will be because of network effects.

This chapter will detail how Web 3.0 will revolutionize the internet in the following sections.

WEB 3.0 AND WHAT IT MEANS FOR THE ECONOMY AND FINANCIAL SERVICES

Networks that are open, trustless, and have no restrictions.

Current internet services are being phased out in favor of a fourth generation. It took over a decade to move from Web 1.0 to Web 2.0, and it's possible that Web 3.0 will take even longer to come to fruition. Powered by machine-based data understanding, Web 3.0 will enable websites and applications to become intelligent, connected and transparent.

Smart homes, where everything from an air conditioner to a light bulb can be controlled from afar, are already showing early signs of Web 3.0. Using Internet of things (IoT) technology, we can now communicate with any connected device in real-time.

Open, trustless, and permissionless are the hallmarks of Web 3.0. Open-source software will be used by an open and accessible community of developers to create Web 3.0, which is why it is called "open." As a second point, the Web 3.0 network will allow people to communicate publicly or privately without the need for a trusted third party. Finally, Web 3.0 will be a permissionless network, requiring no governing body to oversee it.

The emergence of mobile, social, and cloud technologies sparked the second wave of Web 2.0. Edge computing, decentralized data networks, and artificial intelligence (AI) will form the backbone of Web 3.0.

Services powered by artificial intelligence (ML algorithms)

Let's take a closer look at the components that make up Web 3.0. AI and machine learning will be at the heart of Web 3.0. Using these technologies, the Web 3.0 network will be able to leverage decentralized structured data, allowing for meaningful insights and predictions. Precision manufacturing, targeted advertising, drug development, and climate modeling are just some of the many possible uses for this technology.

Web 3.0's increased computing power will be made possible in large part by AI/ML. Through computer vision and natural language processing, artificial intelligence will allow machines and devices to comprehend the non-digital world. Web 3.0 will be powered by AI's ability to keep learning and improving its program, which will allow for personalized experiences for users.

Decentralized data architecture

Web 3.0 has the potential to truly open up the internet to the masses. Making it open and decentralized is one of the primary ways to do it. A decentralized structure allows data to be stored on a variety of interconnected devices, each of which serves a specific purpose, such as a node or verifier or developer, in the network. Because the data is encrypted and time-stamped, it cannot be tampered with or hacked by any of the devices in the system.

Blockchain technology is used to power these capabilities. There is a copy of the data ledger on every connected device, and any change to the data must be approved by all the nodes in the structure. As a result, gaining access to all of the connected devices at once is both difficult and costly.

Edge computing infrastructure

In order for 5G to reach its full potential, the infrastructure provided by edge computing is necessary. The latency between a device and a cloud-based processor will be greatly reduced with 5G's speeds, which are 100 times faster than those of 4G. There are now 58 countries in the world where 5G has been deployed as of June 2021, compared to just 38 countries in 2020. 5G services are expected to be used by 1 billion people in 3.5 years.

Computing tasks will be performed closer to, if not directly on, the data collection site with the help of edge computing infrastructure. It will enable edge servers, cameras, and even smartphones to run facial recognition algorithms in real-time, unlocking supercomputer processing power everywhere.

It is predicted that Web 3.0 will fundamentally change the way we interact with both humans and machines. Using Web 3.0, we will be able to communicate with anyone or anything in the world without the need for fee-charging intermediaries.

WEB 3.0 IN FINANCIAL SERVICES

Toward the end of this century, the internet will become more decentralized and personalized than it is today. Exactly what does this imply for the financial sector? With large funds, banks and other traditional institutions will soon be able to compete with FinTech companies, but they will have a long way to go before they do. It is imperative that financial institutions begin investing in and enhancing their in-house technology capabilities as soon as possible. Collaboration and partnership will be essential, and we are already seeing this.

The emergence of AI and ML

AI IS BEING USED by financial institutions to generate new revenue streams, reduce costs, and streamline labor-intensive procedures. The majority of those working in the financial services industry is also very optimistic about the potential applications of artificial intelligence (AI). According to a recent NVIDIA survey, more than eight out of ten financial professionals (83 percent) agreed that AI is important for the future success of their company.

Depending on the type of financial firm, the approach to using AI varies. Most financial technology and investment companies use AI primarily for algorithmic trading, fraud detection, and portfolio optimization rather than for more general applications. Banks use AI primarily for fraud detection, recommendation systems, and sales and marketing improvement. Finally, for consumer banks, AI is not only used for fraud detection and prevention but also for customer acquisition and retention, as well as cross-selling and up-selling of personalized products and services.

As a result of the bank's private AI training, the bank has reduced customer calls and delivered new applications more quickly to its clients. Meanwhile, BNY Mellon, the world's largest provider of cross-border payment services, has trained its AI and ML models to predict fraud, increasing its accuracy by 20%. By analyzing real-time market data in nanoseconds, AI and high-performance computing are combined to provide traders with better and faster intelligence.

However, the FinTech industry has seen the most ground-breaking advancements in AI. Mortgages and insurance are among the financial products that NerdWallet uses ML to recommend to its customers. In order to improve its ability to match NerdWallet's members with the right products, its recommendation engine is being fed with a slew of profile features, including credit scores, outstanding balances, and credit utilization.

The rise of cryptocurrencies and decentralized finance platforms

To DESCRIBE financial products and services that anyone with an internet connection can access, we use the term "decentralized finance" (DeFi). As a result, there is no centralized authority that can block payments or deny access to anything in these products and services.

If Web 3.0 is decentralized and uses blockchain technology, DeFi has the potential to play a much larger role than it does today. However, we can expect a convergence of the Centralized Finance (CeFi) and Decentralized Finance (DeFi) worlds in the near future. CeFi and DeFi are the two financial service providers that are most likely to make significant advancements in financial services innovation.

With DeFi, traditional finance pain points like inaccessibility to bank accounts or financial services; concerns about financial services being brought down by governments or central institutions; premium and hidden charges; risk and delay due to internal human processes can all be eliminated.

As far as I know, how does DeFi work? DeFi provides services without the involvement of banks or other financial institutions through the use of cryptocurrencies and smart contracts. A smart contract in DeFi eliminates all reliance on a financial institution right away. Using a smart contract, money can be transferred or refunded between accounts without the involvement of a financial institution.

DeFi has a slew of potential applications, and that list is growing all the time. There's no better way to manage your entire financial portfolio than with a system that allows you to send and receive money from all over the world while also allowing you to stream it.

THE EVOLUTION OF WEB 3.0 CAPITAL MARKETS

In the wake of the development of blockchain technology, computer scientists who worked on it have become experts in capital markets. When it comes to digital goods and services, there is no need for a third-party payment service provider to facilitate the transaction. Peer-to-peer digital service, powered by peer-to-peer digital money.

Using Bitcoin, we can ensure the integrity of our currency's digital representation because the data or memory that it represents is preserved and cannot be altered. Meanwhile, fiat currency, also known as "hard currency," is being manipulated in ways that have never been seen before. The ongoing pandemic and the aftermath of the Global Financial Crisis have forced central banks to significantly increase the size of their balance sheets. Because of the large quantities of currency being printed, there is little doubt that our money will lose its true value. A Bitcoin-based global financial system may keep the purchasing power of cash or Bitcoin much higher than current fiat-based local financial systems, which tend to lose purchasing power each year.

People now have the ability to claim ownership of their online creations thanks to the advent of Bitcoin. Blockchains will be the foundation for Web 3.0. It's safe to say that Bitcoin is the most secure blockchain at the moment. Bitcoin can be used as a source of security for Web 3.0 applications. Web 3.0 apps and cryptocurrencies are built on the same technology. Using the same private keys, users will be able to own both digital currencies and internet assets, eliminating the artificial divide between money and data. This will allow a unified digital society to emerge.

A high-end graphics processing unit (GPU) is required to solve a mathematical equation faster than other miners, which requires massive computational power.

When it comes to Web 3.0, communities don't own or profit from their contributions. As a result, community-based economies of scale may be possible, ensuring that the power and data of the internet are not controlled solely by large corporations. Participation in Web 3.0's decentralized world is open to everyone, and the more participants there are, the more everyone succeeds. With the goal of increasing community collaboration, more institutional adoption of crypto is needed.

ICOs and STOs (Security Token Offerings) are becoming increasingly popular ways to raise money. Startups and large corporations have a lot in common: IPOs and ICOs. By selling tokens to investors in exchange for an equity stake in the company, they help startups raise money. Over the course of 2017, 92 ICOs raised a total of $1.25 billion. Oliver Bussmann, a former chief information officer at UBS and now the head of a FinTech advisory firm, is confident that ICOs will continue despite government criticism. A new digital business model based on blockchain technology, which combines crowd-funding and (a) a new hybrid asset class of equity ownership and currency, will continue to thrive as the digital way of doing business.

For small business financing, ICOs offer a strong value proposition. It is faster to implement ICOs than other public offerings for small businesses, and it allows them to diversify their sources of funding by not only appealing to investors on the basis of their profit potential but also on the basis of other aspects of their project. ICOs also give small businesses direct access to a seemingly endless pool of potential investors.

WHOLESALE BANKING WITH WEB 3.0

Joining the decentralized economy results in process efficiencies.

KYC compliance and payment management are two areas where banks are still stumbling. Duplicate work between banks and other third parties is common in KYC requests, which typically take 30 to 50 days to process. KYC compliance involves not only a significant investment of time but also a significant financial outlay. Banks are having a harder time staying in compliance because there are so many different regulations and no universally accepted standards. As a result, the entire KYC process becomes a time-consuming and risky undertaking because of large penalties for non-compliance.

As a result, the use of blockchain-based KYC aims to significantly reduce administrative costs for intermediaries. You don't have to re-enter all of your personal information again if you store your KYC documents on a blockchain, which is secure and accessible by other institutions. The blockchain network verifies and confirms a customer's KYC information, reducing the bank's administrative burdens and costs.

To further reduce their concerns about security and privacy, customers save time by only submitting their KYC documents once to the bank. With 1,125 member banks, SWIFT has developed a KYC registry system where KYC data is stored, shared, and regularly checked for updates by SWIFT, the world's leading provider of secure financial messaging services.

Managing insurance and bonds with blockchain

There is a scramble among health and life insurance companies to integrate blockchain technology into their value chain. The most pressing questions revolve around whether blockchain can help insurers reduce costs, manage risk, improve customer service, and ultimately grow their business. Blockchain can have a positive impact on the health and insurance industry in the following areas:

- It is critical for the insurance industry to take advantage of blockchain's ability to encrypt and provide open and transparent access to patient health records.
- It's possible to automate the collection of data and the execution of smart contracts using Blockchain to enable communication among all stakeholders, uniting them on a single network. A lot of time would be saved in the back office by doing this.
- Approximately $80 billion is spent each year by the insurance industry on fraudulent claims. The smart contracts built into the blockchain make it possible to verify the validity of insurance claims.

In 2018, the World Bank issued and managed the world's first blockchain bond, dubbed bond-i, using blockchain technology. The A$110 million ($82.37 million) two-year bond was a huge success, showing that investors are willing to push for the adoption of new technologies in the capital markets. In light of the positive response to the first round of blockchain bonds, the World Bank raised an additional $108 million by issuing another round in 2019.

The bond market can benefit greatly from the use of blockchain technology. The ability of blockchain to lower participation thresholds for bond denominations and simplify the process of participation are two key value propositions in terms of technicality. Since physical documentation is no longer required prior to issuance, thanks to blockchain, the post-trade settlement process involves fewer counterparties and less time and effort.

Blockchain technology has the potential to revolutionize capital markets in emerging economies by reducing costs and intermediaries. Small and medium-sized businesses would have a much better chance of finding funding if this were to happen.

Additionally, the ongoing pandemic is making a strong case for the digitalization of the legacy bond issuance system. During the pandemic, many companies attempted to raise capital.

Due to the slow and human-dependent bond-issuing process, many people had difficulty. There is no doubt that this system can be modernized with the help of blockchain.

Disruption to traditional capital rising

The capital markets are being increasingly disrupted by blockchain technology. Alternative methods of raising capital are now more readily available. For startups, ICOs have been a godsend in raising capital. Startups are raising enormous amounts of money by allocating equity to each coin offering. Also, registering an ICO is cheaper than registering an IPO in terms of legal fees. Startups such as Filecoin, Tezos, EOS and Bancor have been able to raise hundreds of millions of dollars in their first year. In addition, investors have begun to purchase ICOs because they allow them to cash out much earlier than a traditional investment. ICO Investing

In 2018, Telegram raised $1.7 billion in a private ICO, making it the largest ICO to date.

Enhancing existing operations with DeFi

An existing business model can be augmented by the addition of cryptocurrency or DeFi elements. A third-party vendor can be used to enable crypto payments, such as bitcoin, without putting it on a company's balance sheet. Gaining new customers and increasing the size of each sale are the most immediate benefits. Cryptocurrency should be integrated into operations and the treasury function in a more hands-on approach.

It is also possible to use the DeFi platform for a wide range of applications, including asset management and DAOs, as well as lending and borrowing, gaming and insurance and decentralized exchanges, data and analytics, margin trading, staking and tokenization because of its permissionless and programmable nature, as well as its immutability and interoperability.

DeFi's potential adoption in the financial sector is boosted by its unique combination of cryptocurrency and blockchain features. Transparency and decentralization ensure that financial services are not vulnerable to large-scale hacks, according to Gwyneth Iredale, who is a blockchain software evangelist. As a side benefit, the immutability of DeFi protocols prevents unauthorized access to private financial data.

REMEMBER: Because of the rapid advancements in AI and machine learning that will be enabled by Web 3.0, an enormous amount of previously untapped data will be made readily available for analysis. New markets, new business models, and a slew of other possibilities will result as a result of this. It could be interpreted as a "return to the global village," which is a valid interpretation.

Blockchain technology will be at the heart of Web 3.0. A convergence of cutting-edge technologies will bring Web 3.0 to a level of efficiency that has never been achieved before, as blockchain continues to improve and eliminates inefficiencies across nearly everything it touches. Acknowledging, understanding and mitigating these risks will be prudent in this situation.

Financial services and other industries will undergo a major shift in the coming years. Even new markets and customer segments will be opened up by Web 3.0. COVID-19 serves as a timely reminder of the possibilities opened up by modern technological advancements. Once again, on a global scale, it has been demonstrated that technological innovation and adoption are essential for survival. When Web 3.0 finally arrives, organizations will need to be ready to take advantage of the opportunities it presents.

Web 3.0's emphasis on digital freedom is a significant shift from the current Web 2.0 model. At least theoretically, this new wave of decentralization will allow users to take control of a network. Even if it sounds like a good idea, it comes with a lot of responsibility and can be difficult for both organizations and individuals.

Web 3.0 is on its way, and there are plenty of opportunities in store for those who seize the moment. It's up to us to figure out how to use it for the greater good and keep innovating. We'll probably be talking about Web 3.0 in various ways in a few years, but in order to take part and benefit from this new era, we need to get ready for it now.

CHAPTER 11
THE FUTURE OF WEB 3.0
AND THE METAVERSE

Some of the coverage of Web3 (also known as web 3.0) and metaverse has led some to believe that they refer to the same thing, which is understandable given the amount of hype and excitement they have generated. It is true that they are related in many ways, but this does not mean they describe the same concept. First, let's take a look at the differences between these two terms.

To put it simply, web3 is the internet that isn't owned by any one person or company but rather is built on distributed technologies like the blockchain and decentralized autonomous organizations (DAOs).

The goal is to make the Internet more democratic. When a network is running on hardware owned by a single entity, no single entity can control the flow of information or "pull the plug" to shut it down. User-owned servers and systems are expected to be in place in the future, allowing users to vote on what rules and regulations are put in place and how they are implemented. What's the deal with the name "web3?" In addition to the worldwide web (web1) and user-generated web, this is expected to be the third major internet evolution (social media or web2).

ARE WEB 3.0 AND METAVERSE THE SAME THING?

For a variety of reasons, they are often referred to as one and the same. It's important to note that despite my statements above, no one really knows what either of them is yet.

It's hard to tell what they will look like when they're finished because they're being built by so many different people and organizations. At least $10 billion is expected to be spent on developing the concept of a metaverse by Meta (formerly Facebook) in 2021. But its vision of the metaverse is very different from those who believe the metaverse should be decentralized and outside of the control of big corporations – like Meta.

Web 3.0 has been used to refer to both the decentralized web (web3) and the metaverse, both of which represent the third major iteration of the internet. Web3 is a term you can search on Google right now and get a lot of results that refer to what I described in the first paragraph of this article. However, "the immersive web" – a new generation of the web that is primarily differentiated from what previously existed by its "immersiveness" – has been described as "web 3.0." To put it another way, the metaverse!

Third, and perhaps most crucially, there are some significant overlaps between the two, which leads to confusion. We will be able to use the virtual worlds of the metaverse for everything from work to play to socializing and learning thanks to the web3 technology, which includes blockchain, cryptocurrencies like Bitcoin and Ethereum, and NFTs – unique digital "objects" that are stored on a blockchain.

WEB 3.0 AND THE METAVERSE: HOW WILL THEY COME TOGETHER?

Many people believe that the foundations of economic and financial systems could be laid by cryptocurrency. A digital version of our world, the metaverse, is likely to attract people who want to shop, make money, and start businesses.

People can trade and invest currency tokens that they own without the need for banks, clearinghouses, brokerages, or exchanges (in the traditional sense). All you'd need to outfit your avatar for success in these brave new worlds is a wallet saved on your computer (or in the cloud).

The question is, what would you want to buy in the metaverse, and why would anyone want to buy digital items that aren't even "real." Nonetheless, there is already a $54 billion market for in-game items in video games. Most of these items are used by players to decorate their avatars, their in-game homes, or just for the sake of showing off their accomplishments in the game.

Non-fungible tokens (NFTs) come into play here. Additionally, NFTs make it possible for unique items to exist in digital worlds as a key component of the web3 vision. A token on an encrypted blockchain makes it impossible to "copy and paste" like most other digital data on the internet, social media, or virtual worlds, which can be infinitely replicated by using "copy and paste."

As a result, companies like Nike are already developing NFT-backed footwear and apparel that can only be purchased digitally. People spend hundreds of dollars on limited-edition sneakers in the real world, so why shouldn't they do the same in the virtual world?

Last but not least, web3 allows for the foundations of digital worlds to be built on decentralized platforms, which is exciting from a technologist's perspective. The Ethereum blockchain, for example, is the foundation of an entire universe called Decentraland. To put it another way, the Ether virtual currency can be used to buy land that is intrinsically yours and not owned by a corporation that owns the servers where you store it. These people have the power to regulate the land's use, which means they can make money from its appreciation as well as impose their own rules about what can and cannot happen there. Through the use of smart contracts – rules that are built into the blockchain and designed to run autonomously – decentralized virtual worlds can implement democratic governance. Physicists, you may not like the fact that the laws of physics prevent you from hopping continents. Think the terms and conditions do not adequately protect users from cyber-bullying or hate speech, for example. Start a campaign to get people to vote for the changes you want. A far cry from the digital dictatorships in which corporations set the rules, and we must either accept them or leave the platform in favor of another.

So, there you have it – a quick rundown of how web3 and metaverse differ conceptually but are also intertwined in many ways. Furthermore, both have the potential to help the other grow into a better person, which is why the possibilities for their interaction are so intriguing.

Now, let's look at the future of both Web 3.0 and the Metaverse.

WEB 3.0 AND THE METAVERSE – THE FUTURE

Now that we've reviewed the various Web 3.0 and Metaverse definitions and comparisons, we must ask: How will Web 3.0 and the Metaverse work together in the future?

There should be no single entity that has control over users' data or assets in an "open and decentralized" metaverse. Most early-stage metaverses appear to be owned by different service providers at this point in time. With Facebook's rebranding as "Meta" and the hiring of 10,000 people to work on the Metaverse, some have argued that it's simply a ploy to distance the company from recent scandals surrounding data security and user privacy. For the most part, Facebook's entry into the Metaverse has been a positive one, bringing in $50 million in capital and 10,000 new jobs to help build the infrastructure of the Metaverse, as well as making the idea of it more widely accepted in the mainstream.

Users' digital identities and content created on platforms like Facebook are stored in centralized servers over which they have no control because companies like Facebook are centralized identity providers. As a result, these firms serve as both technology providers and decision-makers, in addition to being the owners of the data they collect.

As we've seen over the last few years, tech companies aren't always the best stewards of our personal information and the interests of their customers. It is critical that the implementation of decentralization and user ownership be prioritized, and this can be achieved through the set of rules and guidelines provided by Web 3.0, as many new entrants to the metaverse market sketch out their future visions for the Metaverse.

Metaverse and Web 3.0 are perfect complements to one another. In spite of the fact that Web 3.0 favors a decentralized web, the Metaverse could serve as a foundation for connectivity there. As an alternative, Metaverse's creator economy can enhance Web 3.0's vision by creating an entirely new financial landscape through the use of decentralized solutions.

What kind of internet do we want to emphasize in the Metaverse as we move towards decentralized Web 3.0? Due to the Metaverse's focus on bringing the virtual and physical worlds together, an open-source public chain is essential for interconnecting different virtual worlds, transferring assets between them, and allowing them to overlap seamlessly.

Despite the rapid growth of NFTs, P2E games, and DAOs in recent months, there is still a long way to go before the full development of the Metaverse and a lot of room for growth in terms of technology that will make the metaverse experience truly immersive.

New open and decentralized world realities appearing in virtuality will be manifested in the Web 3.0 Metaverse. I'm excited to see what the future holds for Web 3.0 and the Metaverse!

CHAPTER 12
INVESTING IN THE
METAVERSE

In 2021, the world and the tech industry as a whole began to recover. In 2021, there were more revolutionary developments in the world of technology. A new standard for digital asset ownership has been set by non-fungible tokens (NFTs) and mainstream crypto solutions. However, in 2022, one of the most hotly debated topics in the tech landscape will have a profound effect on the future of technology.

Metaverse, the three-dimensional version of the internet, is attracting a lot of interest from those looking for ways to invest. However, keep in mind that the metaverse is still a work in progress. There are currently a number of metaverse platforms that offer a variety of virtual experiences. Considering the time it may take before you see a fully functional metaverse, you should be cautious before exploring investment opportunities in the metaverse.

What are your options for putting money into the metaverse? Investing your hard-earned money in the metaverse: Is there a safe way to do it? The following discussion provides an outline of proven methods for making investments in the metaverse, which you can use to find the answers to your questions.

WHY INVEST IN THE METAVERSE?

For starters, because of its close ties to the blockchain and cryptocurrency, metaverse has the potential to be a good investment platform. The metaverse relies on smart contracts and NFTs to facilitate the purchase and exchange of goods between different virtual spaces within the metaverse. NFTs and metaverse crypto are ideal investment instruments for those who want to invest in the various metaverse platforms.

In addition, metaverse platforms like Decentraland and Sandbox, where virtual real estate deals can be made, show the future growth potential of the metaverse. It has been estimated that the metaverse market opportunity is around $1 trillion. It's no surprise that many leading technology firms are investigating metaverse investment opportunities, given its enormous potential.

THE BEST WAYS TO INVEST IN THE METAVERSE

Everyone is wondering how to invest in metaverse crypto with the assurance of the best returns because of the metaverse's growing popularity. Tech companies and institutional investors are putting their money where their mouth is in the metaverse space. However, a lack of information about the various investment options may be a problem for the average investor before he or she decides to invest in the metaverse. Here are a few tried-and-true strategies for making the most of metaverse investment opportunities.

Buy Metaverse Tokens

Investing in metaverse tokens is one of the simplest ways to do so. The purchase of metaverse tokens does not require any complicated steps, which is an interesting feature. You can buy the native tokens of the metaverse platform in which you wish to invest. The following metaverse tokens are currently the most popular: AXS, SAND, and MANA.

AXS is the primary token of Axie Infinity metaverse. SAND is the primary token of Sandbox metaverse. Finally, MANA is the primary token of Sandbox metaverse.

Investing in the metaverse can be made easier if investors use metaverse tokens, which are the primary form of payment in the metaverse. MANA's market value was $4.11 billion at the time of this writing. The value of metaverse tokens is expected to rise in line with the increased adoption of the metaverse. However, like cryptocurrencies, the value of metaverse tokens can fluctuate. As a result, by purchasing metaverse tokens as an investment, investors in the metaverse assume the risk of fluctuating token prices.

Purchase In-game NFTs or Virtual Land

The metaverse's investment opportunities now include virtual real estate, which has risen to prominence. You can create and trade assets and intuitive experiences in metaverse environments that resemble those found in video games. On metaverse platforms, you can learn how to invest in the metaverse using in-game NFTs and virtual land parcels.

Purchase NFTs and virtual land by signing up for a metaverse account. It's easy to buy or sell virtual land in Decentraland, buy or sell NFT art in Sandbox, and sell NFT characters and virtual land parcels in Axie Infinity, for example.

In addition, investing in the metaverse via NFTs and virtual land comes with some serious consequences. The value of non-fungible tokens isn't predetermined and can be affected by a variety of variables, such as scarcity. But there are advantages and disadvantages to purchasing NFT or virtual land parcels through primary and secondary NFT marketplaces.

It is possible to guarantee a higher resale value for NFTs on primary NFT marketplaces, such as the metaverse platforms. Investors, on the other hand, may have difficulty determining the true value of NFTs in the primary market. Secondary marketplaces such as OpenSea ensure that you can compare prices and access information about all NFTs.

What's more, the increasing popularity of virtual real estate shows that investing in metaverse crypto can be made simple. Many businesses are pouring millions of dollars into securing a stake in digital territory. Pavia, an NFT project, recently sold out 60 percent of its 100,000 virtual land parcels available for sale.

You can't miss out on Decentraland, which has a circulation of nearly 36 million MANA. Sandbox is a metaverse where celebrities like Snoop Dogg are creating virtual properties. Because of these factors, virtual land NFTs and in-game NFTs look promising as investment opportunities.

ALTERNATIVE METAVERSE INVESTMENT

The metaverse offers a simple investment opportunity. It is possible to experiment with simpler investment strategies in the metaverse. The following are some good ideas for investments in the metaverse.

Exchange-Traded Funds (ETF)

ETFs should be noted among the many answers to the question, "What is the best way to invest in the metaverse?" You can buy a collection of stocks that are dynamically traded by a dedicated fund manager in a metaverse ETF. With an ETF, you get a single asset with predictable returns by curating a group of similar or thematically organized stocks. A dedicated fund manager is responsible for actively trading the ETF and maintaining its optimal market value, whereas mutual funds do not have such a manager.

Diversified assets are a simple way to lower volatility and, as a result, exposure to risk. Roundhill Ball Metaverse ETF is a notable ETF platform for investing in the metaverse. Investing in the ETF can be done through a brokerage account. There is currently the largest ETF fund focusing on computer hardware, gaming and IaaS solutions, as well as cloud computing.

Metaverse Stocks

IT'S possible to invest indirectly in metaverse by purchasing the stock of a company that's engaged in metaverse development. Investments in gaming and 3D technology companies in the metaverse ecosystem are highly lucrative. Roblox, a metaverse gaming stock, is an option for investors.

Although it started out as a standard video game, it has since evolved into something entirely new, similar to the metaverse. Roblox shares have a promising user base of 47 million, making them a viable investment option in the metaverse. The other option is to invest in the stock of companies that develop metaverse 3D technologies, such as NVIDIA.

Investments in Metaverse Index

"How can I invest in the metaverse indirectly?" is a common question, and the only answer is the Metaverse Index (MVI). Like stock market indices, the Metaverse Index measures the performance of a country's leading companies. The mission of MVI is to keep tabs on the latest developments in the virtual worlds of business, gaming, and entertainment. One of the advantages of investing in metaverses through MVI is that it has lower volatility. To put it another way, investing in the MVI has a lower chance of losing money than investing in metaverse tokens.

Sell or Rent Metaverse Experiences

Among "how to invest in metaverse crypto" solutions, the final recommendation focuses on the experience in the metaverse. Virtual land parcels can be customized and rented out for businesses or offices. Investing in the metaverse can also include renting out billboards on metaverse property for advertising purposes.

As a whole, investments in the metaverse are seen as simple and easy to make using simple methods. Purchase metaverse tokens from one of the top metaverse platforms using a cryptocurrency wallet you've set up. NFTs and virtual land parcels can also be purchased by investors to invest in a specific metaverse platform.

Metaverse investors can, on the other hand, invest in metaverse company stock and exchange-traded funds. It is still in its infancy, but the metaverse has a lot of room to grow in the future. Investors in the metaverse should do their homework before making any decisions about their investments.

THE BEST METAVERSE STOCK TO BUY

As previously stated, it could be many years before the metaverse is fully realized. Companies that are already doing well but will see an acceleration in growth as a result of the metaverse are the best metaverse stocks to buy right now. In no particular order, here are some of the most important considerations:

1. Meta

Facebook, formerly known as Meta Platforms (NASDAQ:FB), ushered the metaverse trend into investors' consciousness. Almost all of Facebook and Instagram's revenue comes from advertising. Meta Platforms, on the other hand, has a division called Reality Labs that specializes in the sale of VR hardware and content. As a result of the success of its Oculus VR headset, Meta has become the most popular stock in immersive technology. The company is spending billions on developing augmented reality and virtual reality software and content, allowing it to look at the metaverse from a variety of perspectives.

2. Unity

It is clear that Unity (NYSE:U) is the undisputed king of the 3D software market. Most 3D content is now created using software developed by this company. It's reasonable to expect that a significant portion of the metaverse content will involve Unity in some way. The company's unique value proposition makes it likely to continue eroding market share from rivals. Unity offers two of its products, Unity Personal and Unity Student, for free to newcomers. Eventually, these up-and-coming designers will be able to afford Unity's services.

3. Nvidia

Nvidia is another company that has the potential to profit from the creation of 3D content (NASDAQ:NVDA). Many companies and content creators are already considering the Omniverse Enterprise product that was made available in late 2021, even though it hasn't yet been released to the public. Nvidia stands to gain from the metaverse trend even if Omniverse ultimately fails to gain traction. Since its inception, the company has focused on developing high-quality graphics processing units (GPUs), which will be in high demand as the metaverse trend continues to grow.

4. Cloudflare

Cloudflare (NYSE:NET) is a content delivery network (CDN) built for speed. Almost all of the world's population is covered by the company's network, which it claims can deliver content within 50 milliseconds or less. As the metaverse expands, this scale will come in handy. Cloudflare, on the other hand, can help with some of the metaverse's other requirements. For example, the company already provides cybersecurity solutions, preventing 117 billion threats per day from reaching the internet. Additionally, in 2021, it launched a data storage product that could help meet the metaverse's enormous data storage needs.

5. Roblox

As a popular virtual world, Roblox (NYSE:RBLX) has the potential to develop into a metaverse platform in its early stages. Virtual concerts have already been hosted by musicians like Tai Verdes and Lil Nas X on Roblox's platform, perhaps signaling that virtual events are becoming more popular with the general public. At first, the platform was most popular with children under the age of 13, but it has since grown into a global company with a growing number of older users around the world. The metaverse is likely to have multiple interactive platforms, but Roblox has a big lead with more than 54 million active daily users.

METAVERSE CRYPTOCURRENCY INVESTMENT

People can shop, play games, buy and trade currencies and objects, and more in a virtual world powered by Metaverse. Consider it a hybrid of augmented reality, virtual reality, social media, gaming and cryptocurrencies.

Cryptocurrencies will be used as currency in the metaverse. Blockchain technology underpins this. When you think about it, "metaverse crypto" comes to mind. Transactions in a given metaverse project can only be made using the project's unique set of tokens.

Fortunately, coin prices are low because metaverse projects are still relatively new, with some going for as little as a few cents in some cases. This widens the range of potential investors. Not every project will be worth your money, however.

This bear market is expected to weed out "bad actors"— developers who have been more concerned with building their fortunes than their projects—according to CNBC.

You should buy metaverse coins that have demonstrated their potential for performance, utility or powerful financial backing.

Here are some promising metaverse cryptocurrency tokens to invest in.

1. ApeCoin (APE)

Tokens known as ERC-20 tokens can be found on the Ethereum blockchain, and APE is one of them. Owners of Apecoin can participate in the governance of the Ape ecosystem and gain access to games and other services that are only available for holders of Apecoin.

Otherside, a Yuga Labs-created metaverse game uses Apecoin as its native token, which is why the Bored Apes Yacht Club tokens are so popular. Otherside token holders recently had the opportunity to purchase parcels in Yuba Labs' virtual land sale, which netted the company $320 million, Fortune reported.

Holders bought 55,000 "Otherdeeds," of which 45,000 went to third parties like Yuba Labs NFT owners and project developers. As a result of the sale, Ethereum's "gas fees" — the fee each user pays to conduct a transaction over Ethereum — increased dramatically.

Issues with the minting process of the Otherdeeds caused a significant drop in the apecoin's price and a significant drop in demand, according to Coin Telegraph. The price of APE has dropped from $26 to $3.49 since the sale was announced.

In order to raise the price of APE, it is being taken out of circulation. There is no way of knowing if that will work. It's possible to make a lot of money if the project succeeds by purchasing APE at its current bargain-basement price. The apecoin will be worthless if the project fails.

At the time of its launch, Apecoin was expected to have 30 percent of its maximum supply in circulation. If you look at the market capitalization of apecoin (apecoin's market capitalization is $1.015 billion), it is the fourth largest metaverse coin.

2. Sandbox (SAND)

The Sandbox, a crypto metaverse project, has performed admirably thus far. Last November, SAND was trading at $8.40, an all-time high for the platform's native token, which had been steadily rising throughout the year.

Although the price has fallen precipitously since then, it is still trading at $0.8613 on June 16th, the same as the majority of cryptocurrencies.

This project is bringing the metaverse vision to life with a virtual reality component. Gaming brands such as Atari have backed The Sandbox, which could help it weather the current market downturn. In addition, Deadline reported that Lionsgate and The Sandbox had recently partnered to create a "Hellboy" metaverse location.

NFTs play a major role in Sandbox's economy. Using the SAND metaverse tokens, players can create non-physical entities (NFTs).

Ethereum is the underlying technology for this project, as is the case with many others.

More promising is that there are only 3 billion coins available, of which 1.24 billion are currently in use. In terms of market capitalization, it is currently valued at $1.07 billion.

3. Decentraland (MANA)

One of the more well-known projects in the crypto metaverse is Decentraland. The NFT craze was a part of the reason, but the platform's native token, MANA, also saw significant gains.

A large number of NFT owners began utilizing the platform to showcase their NFTs. This metaverse platform includes more than just NFTs. You can also buy virtual land and create virtual games and other digital assets, which is how the site got its name.

In Decentraland, the luxury goods and art broker Sotheby's purchased a plot of land and built a replica of its London headquarters. This shows that even large corporations are interested in pursuing metaverse initiatives.

Decentraland, which was founded in 2017, is an older project that has had a hard time gaining traction. Despite its lackluster performance, MANA's market cap of $1.548 billion as of June 16 makes it the largest metaverse token in terms of market cap.

In comparison to where it was a year ago, MANA has dropped significantly.

4. Highstreet (HIGH)

This is an interesting metaverse project with virtual reality support that has some promise in terms of metaverse applications, at least at this point. For starters, the virtual currency HIGH can be used to buy goods and services in the virtual world. Shopify stores have been integrated into the platform already.

As a result, it appears to be up to date on the most recent technological and cryptographic trends. In addition, Coinbase has added HIGH to its list of supported cryptocurrencies.

From a real-world or meta-world perspective, this project has already fulfilled the promise of metaverse technology in this instance. Consider this if you're an investor who values practicality above all else.

HTC is a supporter of the project, which raised $5 million in August 2021. In June 2022, it will have a market value of over $15.83 million.

5. Floki Inu (FLOKI)

There are many dog-meme-based cryptocurrencies out there, but Floki Inu may be the most undervalued of them all. In honor of Elon Musk's Shiba Inu dog, the currency has been renamed Shiba Inu Tokens.

According to the website, the project's goal is to integrate memes with real-world applications. An NFT marketplace and content and education platform are expected to be launched at the same time. Despite the fact that this is a work in progress, investors have continued to purchase FLOKI tokens.

With a market cap of $55.84 million, Floki Inu currently trades on the secondary market for $0.000006172.

6. Metahero (HERO)

Real-world objects and people can be turned into HD avatars for use in the Metaverse through the use of 3D scanning in the Metahero project. Additionally, the company has installed a 3D scanning chamber in Doha in order to scan objects for the Metahero universe.

This is why Metahero has teamed up with Wolf Studio. HERO, its native cryptocurrency token, was valued at $43.36 million in June 2022. Despite the fact that it's smaller than other tokens on this list, this is a relatively new project, so it has a smaller market capitalization.

Compared to other alt-coins, Metahero's YTD performance stands at -93 percent. Metahero could benefit from recent collaborations between CEO Rob Gryn and his other meta-project, *Everdone*.

7. Terra Virtua Kolect (TVK)

When NFTs were still in their infancy, Terra Virtua Kolect was born. NFTs are now the focus of a virtual environment. The native token TVK can be used to create, sell, and buy NFTs from other members.

In light of the recent surge in NFT investment, this project has a lot of potentials. In accordance with CoinMarketCap, the platform can be used in web, PC, and VR/AR environments.

In order to improve the long-term viability of Terra Virtua, the Cardano blockchain was recently integrated. NFT Evening reported that Polygon, the first carbon-positive blockchain, had been integrated into the platform.

TVK's current market capitalization is over $24.41 million, and the company's YTD performance is -85%. Long-term viability may be enhanced by new partnerships, such as the one with NFT game Kawaii Islands, which has just been announced.

8. Star Atlas (ATLAS)

Based on a video game with stunning visuals, Star Atlas is a metaverse project. The game takes place in the distant future of the year 2620, and it allows players to conquer land and gather resources in a sci-fi world.

As part of a recent agreement, the metaverse expects to see a rise in the number of players in Star Atlas thanks to its partnership with PC manufacturer iBuyPower.

In order to participate in the game, you must earn the metaverse token ATLAS. As you play and complete tasks, you'll earn coins, just like in any other reward-based game. It's a different story, however, when it comes to the rewards.

In comparison to Ethereum-based projects, the game is built on Solana, which has a lower transaction fee. It has a market capitalization of just under $13 million and is currently trading at $0.005981 per coin on the exchanges.

9. Enjin (ENJ)

Enjin is no exception to the rule when it comes to metaverse coins. ENJ, the local token, can be "minted" in this metaverse-style gaming environment and used to purchase assets that will help you progress in the game.

It is possible to buy everything in the game, from medicine to character upgrades, with ENJ tokens. As a result, it's akin to a market.

The Ethereum blockchain powers Enjin, which currently has a market cap of $392.578,000. There are currently more than 100 games and apps available in Enjin's NFT parachain on Polkadot.

To celebrate the milestone of 500,000 users' wallets, Enjin is gearing up to begin beta testing version 2.0 of their popular app, the Enjin Wallet, very soon.

10. Epik Prime (EPIK)

NFTs have become the focus of Epik Prime, a metaverse project. PancakeSwap, Hotcoin Global, KuCoin, and Huobi Global all offer EPIK as a cryptocurrency. Over 300 gaming clients and licensing agreements with Warner Music and Universal suggest that Epik is likely to recover from the recent slump in the cryptocurrency market.

There is a market capitalization of $4.18 million for EPIK, which was released just last year. Even though it's the tiniest coin on this list, major companies have already begun using it, so it's worth looking into. Over 349 million coins, or 17%, of the total supply, are currently in use.

STEP-BY-STEP GUIDE TO INVESTING IN METAVERSE

The tips about how to invest in the metaverse above are the indirect ways of investing in the metaverse. In this section, I will teach you a practical and direct step-by-step guide about how to invest in metaverse smoothly.

STEP 1: Create a Cryptocurrency Wallet

A wallet full of cash is required for every purchase, just like with physical goods. Create a crypto wallet and load it up with virtual currency to invest in the metaverse. Some of the best crypto wallets for metaverse tokens are CoinSwitch Kuber, CoinDCX, and WazirX. These wallets are majorly popular in India.

When it comes to NFT purchases, the best cryptocurrency wallets are MetaMask, Coinbase, and Binance. Since Ethereum is the most common platform for NFTs, it's best to buy ETH with your local currency. Completing the KYC (know your customer) procedures will allow you to validate your wallet and confirm your identity.

STEP 2: Register for an account in your chosen choice of platform

Once you have opened an account, the first thing to do is to buy metaverse tokens. If you have a currency-loaded wallet, you can buy these tokens directly from cryptocurrency exchanges like CoinDCX or WazirX. Metaverse tokens such as the Decentraland metaverse's MANA, the Sandbox metaverse's SAND, and the Axie Infinity metaverse's AXS are all highly sought after. When purchasing in-game NFTs or virtual land, to make purchases in a game, you'll need to sign up for an account and link your crypto wallet to it. On the other hand, if you're interested in buying or selling virtual goods, you can visit Decentraland or Axie Infinity. If you want to access all NFTs in one place, you can sign up for an account with OpenSea.

STEP 3: Choose the NFT you want to buy and pay for it

YOU'LL NOTICE that NFTs don't have a predetermined selling price on any of the above platforms. To own the NFT, one must compete with other bidders and win the highest bid. The wallet you created and loaded with cryptocurrency in Step 1 is used to quickly process your payment for the NFT.

NOTE: Buying from a primary marketplace (Decentraland, Axie Infinity, Sandbox, etc.) or a secondary marketplace (OpenSea, etc.) has both advantages and disadvantages to consider. The resale value of an NFT in the primary market will always be higher. However, determining its true value in the primary market is more difficult. To make it easier to compare the prices of various NFTs, one common platform has been created where all NFTs are displayed.

REMEMBER: There is a slew of new metaverse projects popping up all the time, but only a few have the potential to be truly great. It's a good idea to invest in some of these projects because the metaverse concept is deeply rooted in blockchain and cryptocurrency. As a result, NFT's popularity seems to be on the rise. Don't put all of your money into one metaverse coin, and don't invest money you can't afford to lose, like with any other investment. Investing in coins that you believe have the potential to grow is the best strategy.

CHAPTER 13
METAVERSE: THE FUTURE OF BUSINESS AND INVESTMENT

To say that Metaverse is creation is an understatement. The Metaverse's growth was accelerated by the COVID-19's impact on digital economies and offline business model disruptions when the Meta platform announced its origins. NFTs (Non-fungible Tokens) fueled the demand for Metaverse in the wake of blockchain's rise.

Users can interact and explore with other people who aren't in the same physical location in Metaverse, a virtual reality space. There is a vast ecosystem of gateways, platforms and infrastructure in the Metaverse to enhance the customer experience with identity, social and gaming services. Individual virtual worlds exist, each with its own set of rules for membership, access, and use of monies earned.

A 3D realistic digital world for businesses means the ability to buy, sell, sign, and enforce contracts as well as recruit and interact with customers all over the world. Metaverse makes it simple for customers to try out the company's various digital recreations and products in virtual spaces.

Additionally, companies realize that the consequences of an immersive and decentralized digital world could be enormous, which is why they're eager to experiment with new technologies.

- Adding virtual products to the shopping experience.
- Market physical and digital products and services to gain new information about customers.
- Hardware, software, and user experiences are all advancing.

There is no doubt that the Metaverse is here to stay, so it is time to examine how a metaverse impacts real-world industries.

FINANCIAL SERVICES

Traditional financial services are already interested in utilizing Metaverse's potential for branding and product development in their own unique ways. It is expected that Metaverse will lead to decentralized virtual societies in the near future, which will allow people to transact and engage. There is a direct link between virtual-to-physical financial systems and payments in an ecosystem, and new forms of trading emerge as a result of this development.

By narrowing the gap between the online and offline worlds, AR/VR encourages more customers to participate. A growing number of financial institutions are taking advantage of Metaverse as a hub to help and analyze financial risks, provide precise advice to customers without geographical constraints, and increase the customer experience.

AUTOMOTIVE AND MANUFACTURING

The Metaverse's automotive and manufacturing industries will be transformed by a shared online space powered by AR, VR, and

MR. The creation of an industrial metaverse powered by immersive technology is possible with organically integrated cyber-physical integration. It is possible to have a virtual experience of people working together in the virtual world without having to be on-site through on-site installation and skills training.

As a result, Metaverse can be used by the automotive industry to test various aspects of product design and development. Decision-making and results are recorded on the blockchain using Metaverse, in addition to previous functions.

REAL ESTATE

When it comes to real estate, supply and demand play a role in how much a piece of virtual land or building is worth. Land in the Metaverse is valued based on its location, size, and utility, just like in the real world. You can buy or sell parcels of digital real estate on the metaverse platform by utilizing cryptocurrency.

Real-world activities like trade shows, exhibitions and fashion events can be transformed into digital events like sponsorships and booths as more land parcels are put up for sale.

RETAIL AND CONSUMER BRANDS

Direct communication channels between brands and their customers are becoming more common. For the first time, Metaverse introduces a brand-new concept to help them take advantage of the burgeoning retail market numerous opportunities. Nike, Gucci, Louis Vuitton, and other high-end fashion brands have already begun selling virtual products and collectibles in the Metaverse.

AR technology has made it easier for brands to tell their stories, and Metaverse can take it to a whole new level by immersing consumers in a virtual world where they can examine and evaluate products. It also provides a new platform for brand creators to showcase their brand through highly engaging storytelling that informs and influences purchase decisions.

CORPORATE TRAINING

Immersive technologies like AR and VR are displacing traditional methods of job training. A number of businesses are embracing Metaverse because of its numerous advantages, including faster onboarding and hiring, a virtual tour of the office, job-specific training, and a collaborative workspace.

In what ways can companies and organizations best get ready for the metaverse age?

Familiarity

The Metaverse's concepts are unfamiliar to the majority of businesses. Digital transactions and investments can be difficult to understand for many employees. Provide a person or team with the responsibility of researching and learning about cutting-edge topics like cryptocurrencies and decentralized autonomous organizations (DAOs) and how they apply to your company.

Develop a strategy

Analyze their company's needs and identify gaps and long-term opportunities built around metaverse concepts. There will be many businesses that use a digital resource to work through the key concepts of the Metaverse and implement practical measures such as extending existing services to the Metaverse, developing security and identity infrastructure, and establishing APIs to core systems so that all stakeholders can connect to the platform.

Risk Assessment

Metaverse should be approached cautiously, and a few low-risk use cases such as selling digital versions of physical goods, virtual tours, and launching NFTs to improve brand awareness and customer connections through the metaverse platform should be selected for experimentation.

HOW TO MOVE YOUR BUSINESS INTO THE METAVERSE

As Meta CEO Mark Zuckerberg predicted, it could be five to ten years before the metaverse's most popular features become commonplace in our daily lives. However, a few metaverse aspects are already in existence. Virtual reality headsets, ultra-fast broadband, and always-on digital worlds are already in use, despite the fact that not everyone has access to them.

Every brand, no matter how big or small can reap the rewards of establishing an online presence. This is how you can get started as a pioneer in the metaverse or look for business opportunities in the metaverse if you want.

Find the right platform

Choosing the appropriate platform is the first step in discovering "how to get into the metaverse?" answers. The metaverse is a term that encompasses a wide variety of platforms currently in use. Real estate, gaming, and non-fungible tokens (NFTs) are a few examples of the many different types of digital worlds that exist today. Roblox, a platform with over 49 million active users, is one of the most popular.

Aimed at a younger demographic, Roblox provides access to a wide range of games and other forms of entertainment, including music concerts. Additionally, Fortnite's success can be attributed to a model like this. It has evolved into a virtual hangout where gamers can attend in-game concerts and socialize with one another. Trap music superstars such as Travis Scott and Ariane Grande are included in the lineup.

Brands from across the metaverse have begun collaborating with Fortnite on content marketing, PR campaigns and sponsored events in the game's world. Well-known fashion brands like Gucci and Valentino have begun their metaverse forays, while sportswear giants such as Nike and Adidas have opened virtual shops where customers can purchase NFTs of real-life sneakers and athletic gear.

When aiming for a younger audience, you need to emphasize entertainment, authenticity and creativity as core selling points on Roblox-based platforms such as Minecraft.

This approach is also appropriate for a more sophisticated demographic, such as the residents of Decentraland. Instead of gaming, this virtual world emphasizes the development of digital infrastructures based on the Ethereum blockchain. Users can do things like buying virtual land, planning events, and creating (virtual) objects in this world. Samsung and Sotheby's are just two of the many well-known names that have already established themselves in Decentraland.

Before deciding on a platform, it's a good idea to thoroughly research the most popular metaverses and learn about the audiences they attract, the products and services they need, and how your business can fit into a virtual world.

Boost your online presence

There is no doubt that the vast majority of businesses already have an online presence, be it through a website or social media accounts. It's critical to re-evaluate your current online presence and branding strategies before diving into metaverse business opportunities.

Learn the basics of the online market before entering the new world, as they will be the same rules that apply in the old one.

For example, if you want to start a virtual reality company, you'll need a professional website and a strong social media presence. In order to avoid missing out on opportunities and frustrating your customers, you must maintain an online presence. Keep the information current as well.

Develop AR/VR apps

In order to grow your business, you may have to create or at the very least consider using augmented reality and virtual reality tools. Because of the metaverse's location at the nexus of VR, AR, and AI, it's important to familiarize yourself with these technologies before taking your business online.

75 percent of business leaders plan to use AR/VR by 2023, with global spending expected to increase sixfold by 2025, per a recent survey. Because of this, developing an AR/VR application that allows your customers to get acquainted with the metaverse's various features is a good way to begin adapting to this new reality.

In order to get your metaverse experience off the ground, experiment with VR headsets and other supporting technologies like motion controllers.

AR/VR features are already being tested by several brands in the metaverse. A successful campaign by Zara, for example, allowed users to shop using the AR app. Apps like this one allow customers to hold their phones up to store windows or sensors and see models wearing the brand's products come to life on their screens. Using the app, they can even buy the goods they want. After Chanel and Gucci jumped on the bandwagon, others followed suit.

Focus on your target audience

Once you've established your business in the metaverse, the next step is to determine who your target market is. Your product or service will sell itself if you only market to the right people. Customers will have a positive experience as a result, and they will return.

Instead of trying to capture the attention of everyone in the metaverse, you should concentrate your marketing efforts on the needs and wants of your intended audience.

When developing a blood pressure monitoring system for your metaverse business, you should focus on the elderly because they are more likely to experience blood pressure abnormalities.

Focus on the experience

In the metaverse, customers and clients are looking for an experience, not just a view. Users will enjoy your metaverse business if you make it an experience. Consider displaying your merchandise in more than two dimensions if you plan to open a shop. If you're making a game, you should use controls that mimic real-world movements.

Determine the mood you want to evoke in your intended audience before they even step foot in the door. Users will have a positive experience as a result of this feeling. They'll be more likely to return to your store if you do this. Returning users are more likely to spend more money. Customers are more likely to stick with you if they have an enjoyable experience, so you should aim for that.

Maintain the old ways

In the metaverse, it's important not to rush into doing everything all virtual all the time when transitioning your business. In the metaverse, there is a wide variety of ways to get started. Some of your clients might be ready for it, as it does sound exhilarating. However, the core of good business has always been to meet the needs of the customer. Most customers aren't even close to the launch stage.

Even if you're preparing your company for the future, don't forget about the old ways just yet. For the vast majority of your clients, this is the only viable option. Allow your customers to interact with your brand in more traditional ways.

Remain adaptable

It's impossible to know what's right or wrong until the metaverse has a more defined shape. If you want to succeed in the metaverse, you must be able to adapt your business to the ever-changing nature of virtual worlds.

The metaverse's community can help you test your product virtually, which is why this is a good time to do so. Aside from providing insight into what your customers want, this can help you foresee potential future innovations. Get ready to take your business into the metaverse today by embracing the opportunity to expand in ways you never thought possible before.

A VIRTUAL WORLD WITH META-LIVES, META-SOCIETIES AND META-BUSINESSES

As digital beings with meta-lives, we can exist in these worlds. The metaverse provides us with the ability to have a variety of virtual presences through avatars that will be able to share digital spaces for work or play, to conduct business, exercise, or even socialize. The demographics of humans will be replaced by avatar information in this digital extension of our lives.

Meta-Businesses

We can go after meta-lives (the lives of avatars) once we've established businesses in the metaverse. We can now buy, sell, sublet, and rent internet space in virtual worlds using blockchain and NFTs. Business ventures above and beyond "the business world" will flourish in this fertile economic environment.

Meta-Societies

In decentralized worlds, these societies will thrive. In that society, everyone will be able to design its structure and how it will evolve over time.

Liminal Spaces

You can enter the metaverse through these portals. Virtual worlds allow us to experience a different way of life without ever having to leave the comfort of our own homes. You'll be able to see and go to places that haven't yet been conceptualized as a reality. You, too, will be able to feel and express emotions in due time.

Virtual Events

Planning multiple virtual events is now possible thanks to the digital age. It was estimated that 27 million people watched Ariana Grande's Fortnite concert, which gave some idea of the metaverse's potential audience size. It was possible for Ariana and everyone else to attend the concert from the comfort of their own homes.

It's important to remember that people are more likely to attend a virtual event or venue if they've previously experienced one. Because of this, the more people who are aware of the metaverse, the faster it will be filled.

AUGMENTED REALITY

We've made significant advances in the physical world thanks to augmented reality, thanks in part to the use of interfaces and sensors. As a result of this technology, the metaverse could empower users with a sixth sense that will provide a great deal of information and transform work, processes, and life into journeys and experiences.

When someone wants to do something and needs help from an expert, you can become that expert because a journey will make it possible for you to become that expert. Be sure to keep a detailed itinerary for each trip. Your company should recognize that these trips are for your benefit."

MIRROR WORLDS

Reflections of the real world are augmented in the mirror worlds. Virtual technology and sensors enhance the experience by adding a layer of contextual data and graphical information that helps us navigate our surroundings.

Sensors in technology today are used to measure a variety of things, including light intensity, blood pressure, and emotional states. The creation of virtual bodies using these sensors and haptic systems could be useful in a variety of other fields, such as medicine.

With mirror worlds, we can experiment with new ideas and iteratively refine existing ones for the benefit of our users. Knowledge of data transposition is essential. You must be able to access and manage your own data, as well as that of others.

Lifelogging

Lifelogging is a means of registering oneself in this world. When all the sensors in our environment are taken into account, they'll be able to recreate memories that are more than just images; they'll be able to reproduce the feelings you had at the time. In the television series "Upload," we see a glimpse into the digital future.

OPPORTUNITIES FOR EVERYONE

There will be an infinite number of interconnected virtual communities in this hybrid society. Among the benefits of this is that it will allow the metaverse to provide a wider range of virtual goods and services, including real-world financial transactions. Digital shoes sold for $3.1 million, and a digital Gucci handbag sold for more than $4,000 in just seven minutes, for example. It's not a sci-fi story; these transactions are actually taking place today.

This new form of reality offers a plethora of possibilities for businesses to expand their offerings, including real estate, journey builders, concerts, ceremonies, virtual labs, and a slew of other activities that can be enjoyed in a variety of different ways.

This is where things are going. The hard drive gold rush has arrived. There are only a limited number of spots available, so don't miss out on the opportunity while the stakes are high. A low ticket price and a long-term return could be just what you've been looking for.

CONCLUSION

Congratulations on getting to the end of this amazing book. It is my belief that this book has been able to equip you with the best possible details about the Metaverse and how it can greatly benefit your business. While the Metaverse is still a new concept, it is better to get prepared for it to benefit from its maximum offerings.

The Metaverse is going to be a home for many businesses and organizations in a few years to come. Very soon, we all will live in a virtual world where everything and anything is possible.

Digital innovation is increasing interoperability and creating new digital identities with new rules in order to create more immersive experiences for customers in the digital economy. Customers are constantly confronted with a plethora of options because of the widespread availability of social media and the internet.

There is a global trend toward the metaverse, and the rest of the world is betting on it. Now is the time to present new ideas and ensure that your company does not fall behind the competition by adapting and getting a head start.

REFERENCES

Bruno, A., Pascal, G., & Guillaume, M. (2018). Virtual Reality and Augmented Reality: Myths and Realities. John Wiley & Sons, Inc.

"DeFi and Web 3.0: Unleashing creative juices with decentralized finance," CoinTelegraph, accessed June 25, 2022, https://cointelegraph.com/news/defi-and-web-3-0-unleashing-creative-juices-with-decentralized-finance.

"Impact of Web 3.0 on the FinTech Industry," LendFoundry, accessed June 25, 2022, https://lendfoundry.com/blog/impact-of-web-3-0-on-the-fintech-industry/#:~:text=Web%203.0%20will%20reduce%20the,managing%20seizures%20or%20server%20failures.

Nelson, Z., Leonel, M., & Ana, B. (2012). Virtual Worlds and Metaverse Platforms: New Communication and Identity Paradigms. Information Science Reference.

R. William, B. Alan (2003). Understanding Virtual Reality: Interface, Application, And Design. Morgan Kaufmann Publishers.

S. Randall, L. Stephanie (2014). Virtual, Augmented and Mixed Reality: Applications of Virtual and Augmented Reality. Springer International Publishing Switzerland.

T. Jung, M. Claudia (2018). Augmented Reality and Virtual Reality: Empowering Human, Place and Business. Springer International Publishing.

T. Jung, M. Claudia (2019). Augmented Reality and Virtual Reality: The Power of AR and VR for Business. Springer Nature Switzerland.

"Web 3.0 and the Metaverse," SmartValor, accessed June 24, 2022, https://smartvalor.com/en/news/web-3.0-and-the-metaverse.

"What is Web 3.0: A beginner's guide to the decentralized internet of the future," CoinTelegraph, accessed June 25, 2022, https://cointelegraph.com/blockchain-for-beginners/what-is-web-3-0-a-beginners-guide-to-the-decentralized-internet-of-the-future.